Contents

Glossary   **167**

MUHAMMAD MOJLUM KHAN

ADAPTED BY

IMRAN MOGRA

THE MUSLIM 100

VOL.4

The Lives, Thoughts and Achievements of The Most Influential Muslims In History

The Muslim 100 YA Edition:
The Lives, thoughts and achievements of the
most influential Muslims in History.
Volume 4

First published by Kube Publishing Ltd,
Markfield Conference Centre
Ratby Lane, Markfield,
Leicestershire LE67 9SY

United Kingdom
Tel: +44 (0) 1530 249230
Website: www.kubepublishing.com
Email: info@kubepublishing.com

British Library Cataloguing-in-Publication Data

ISBN 978-1-84774-275-9 Paperback

ISBN 978-1-84774-276-6 Ebook

Cover Design: Amaan Ansari
Typesetting: LiteBook Prepress Services

Calligraphy: M. Swallay Mungly

Introduction

It goes without saying that societies across the world are experiencing changes at a very fast pace. We are living at a time when the world is interconnected, and instant communication has become normal. People who were once at the far corners of the world have virtually been brought together and can communicate immediately, perhaps to know one another better. One of the questions that this book invites you to think about is the extent to which you are aware of and connected to the history of Islam and Muslims. Are you a stranger to these great people who have left everlasting legacies for humanity?

Many educators, both Muslims and others, have realised the need to highlight and celebrate the huge contributions that Muslims have made over the centuries in the development of different subjects which gave the world the knowledge and means to improve life and civilisation. It is important for you to recognise that much of this history was deliberately suppressed, degraded, and doubted. Have you wondered why? In fact, there was a time when such history was absent even among some universities and school syllabuses in may countries. You might want to ponder as to why this significant aspect of Muslim heritage and history of humanity was 'hidden'.

One the reasons may well be that it served the purposes of the powerful who wanted to keep their imperialist strategies and colonisation mission alive. Part of this mission involved the creation of a Muslim mind which felt inferior about itself and devalued its own knowledge, people, heritage, and lifestyle. Looking forward, this trend needs to be reversed, and Muslims need to take their rightful place on the world stage. Muslims and Islam matter. Therefore, it is my sincere hope that educational institutions will include this book in their libraries or as part of the syllabuses to enlighten their learners and to keep Islam's legacy alive.

The contribution of Muslims, as you will read, is a vast field and much has been written about it. Some of it remains in the Arabic language in libraries and in personal collections to be discovered by others and presented to the world. A lot of it has been ruined and continues to be destroyed through neglect, natural loss, modernisation, and wars.

In this book, you will find the fantastic contributions of Muslim scholars to literature, calligraphy, political administration, history, sociology, theology, finance and economy, philosophy, science, architecture, *hadith*, *tafsir*, *aqidah*, music, education, morality, mathematics, astronomy, medicine, chemistry, travel, logic, faith and spirituality. You will marvel at the physical geography of forts, palaces, mosques, mausoleums and libraries. You will also reflect upon some pleasant as well as unpleasant events and behaviours of individuals. This past will offer insights into what happened in previous centuries. As a historian, you will interpret the past for the benefit of the present and future.

You will be surprised with the interesting information about Muslim centres of learning which flourished in Europe, North Africa, the Middle East and Asia. You will come across some of the amazing libraries in Cordoba, Spain, established by generous patrons, which contained hundreds of thousands of books accessible to all. You are about to open the pages of the profiles of kings, saints, nobles, tyrants and people with questionable actions, morals and beliefs.

It has been said that history is a mirror of the people, and it is through this mirror of history that people see themselves and the performance of past peoples. As you turn the pages in this collection, you will encounter the photographic memory that some people had. For example, the compilers of *Hadith* literature memorised thousands of sayings of the Prophet Muhammad (ﷺ) and saved them for future generations. Muslims are forever indebted to them for preserving the lifestyle of the Prophet (ﷺ) for everyone. These narratives inform you about Muslim heritage so that you become conscious of your connections with your predecessors and hopefully give you a sense of direction for your life ahead.

Whilst you curiously examine these biographies, take note of the social history of the time and think about the trade links, commerce, travels, the lifestyle and other social characteristics of these historical periods. There are fascinating gems of information both in terms of facts and figures. Try to learn and remember some of these and share them with others. But you must see beyond these facts and probe into the cause and effects of the rise and fall of nations and their rulers.

Spirituality is a theme that runs through most of the lives of these remarkable people. In whatever they pursued, they did not ignore this critical aspect of their life, their relationship with Allah and their pursuit of achieving higher ideals in life. They always kept, in their mind and heart, the Hereafter as their final destination and prepared for it diligently. But they were not only concerned about themselves. They wished others to be mindful of Allah, to become better people and live in kindness with a view to eternal happiness. How did they achieve this?

These brilliant narratives will illustrate to you the preservation, reformation, revival and propagation of Islam and the different methodologies adopted by scholars, saints, activists, politicians, philanthropists, Imams, shaykhs and soldiers for this. They preserved the light of Islam in a variety of ways. They aimed to beautify (*ihsan*) characters, ethics and manners. They also aimed to purify (*tazkiya*) the heart and soul. They taught (*ta'lim*) knowledge. They converted and disseminated (*da'wah*) the message of Islam.

One of the most fascinating observations to make is that there is a universal characteristic that flows through these people as they belonged to different cultures, races, ethnicities and languages, and that they were rich and poor, male and female. Actually, some were crippled, like Tamerlane, who was one of the world's greatest conquerors, and others were orphaned very young. Yet they achieved great accomplishments. Mothers have been the bedrock for the likes of Imam al-Bukhari and many others, as you will read.

As you study these short biographies, you will notice their sincerity, determination and humility in search of learning. This enabled them to travel to distant lands and sit at the feet of experts with different faiths, cultures and worldviews. In doing so, they learnt other local languages, translated books and critically evaluated other people's knowledge and truth claims. They then made this knowledge widely accessible.

You will also be exposed to some Muslim, Greek and other philosophical thoughts which may appear unfamiliar to you. As you read, you will understand that some of these civilisations are different from the Islamic civilisation, spirituality and morality. However, some understanding of this is necessary, without making generalisations about Western thought and modernism, because these ideals and ideas continue to influence the political, social, ethical, aesthetic and economical thought of the current modern world. You will also encounter the different thoughts and schools that exists among Muslims.

You will recognise that unity and justice were cornerstones for many of those leaders who were more successful in providing stability and security. These then facilitated the establishment of educational centres, hospitals and general public order. Once these were functioning and secure, the wellbeing and prosperity of their peoples and societies followed. On the other hand, exploitation, oppression, greed, nepotism, corruption, deception and disunity brought downfall. In other words, be curious as you dive into the past and arrive at an appreciation about the how and why of events.

You are living at a time when Western civilization and the powers associated with them are at the top. Muslim nations are weaker and controlled but Muslims have spiritual strength. This book will make you realise that the story of Muslims was once different and the direction that the world is taking can be changed. You need to take up this challenge to your heart to lead the world. There is plenty to inspire you and for you to aspire to.

As you have a dialogue with this historical period, I sincerely hope that what you learn from this collection creates a love for further knowledge. I hope you will appreciate these figures' amazing achievements and that their legacy motivates you to greatness and the service of humanity. Nobody ever imagined that Islam, which was on verge of extinction during the night of *hijra,* would spread to all corners of the world and become a religion with over a billion followers. You are about to discover how that happened.

The biographies have been presented in a chronological order. It will help you to place the geography, personalities and events in a systematic order of history. From the school and curriculum perspective to grasp history well, an understanding of its chronology is important. The chronology will support you to develop a better mental framework of the past so that you have a secure grasp of the timeline of Islam as it has unfolded over the centuries. You should also be able to extend and deepen your knowledge and understanding of local and world history. This will provide you with a well-informed context for learning history in general. Register in your mind the younger age at which some of them died but how massive their success and impact has been. Overall, you will identify significant events, make connections, compare and contrast and analyse trends over centuries.

Imran Mogra
July 2025

81

Shaykh Ahmad Sirhindi (b.1564 - d.1624 CE) / (b.972 - d.1034 AH)

The reign of the Mughal Emperor Akbar the Great is generally considered to be the Golden Age of Muslim rule in India. After ascending the Mughal throne during the middle of the sixteenth century, he ruled India for five decades and completely transformed the fortunes of the Mughal dynasty. He expanded Mughal political control across the subcontinent and initiated far-reaching social and cultural reforms throughout that region. In other words, as a military commander and strategist, Akbar was supremely successful, but as a politician and reformer he proved to be controversial, to say the least.

Not surprisingly, his cultural and religious reforms ended up in total shambles. As a religious freethinker, he promoted a form of religious pluralism which upset both Muslims and Hindus. According to the Muslims, Akbar's religious fusion, known as *din-i-ilahi* (the Divine Religion), made a complete mockery of Islamic teachings, while orthodox Hindus considered his religious experimentation to be ill-conceived and bizarre.

Thus, instead of strengthening Hindu-Muslim relations, Akbar's amateurish approach to religious dialogue and debate only served to divide the two communities further. During this critical period in the history of Muslim India, Shaykh Ahmad Sirhindi, a pioneering Sufi thinker and influential Islamic reformer, emerged to defend the cause of traditional Islam. He re-formulated one of the most powerful doctrines of Islamic spiritual philosophy.

Also known as *mujaddid-i alf-i thani* (Renewer of the Second Millennium of Islam), Shaykh Ahmad Sirhindi was born in the town of Sirhind (located in the Indian State of Punjab) into a respected family of religious scholars and Sufi saints. His father, Shaykh Abd al-Ahad, was an important Islamic scholar who claimed to be a descendant of Caliph Umar through his son, Abdullah ibn Umar, the famous narrator of Prophetic traditions. Brought up in a deeply religious family, young Ahmad was encouraged by his father to commit the entire Qur'an to memory before he was ten. He then pursued the standard curriculum of the day which included Arabic, Persian, literature, *fiqh* (Islamic jurisprudence), *Hadith* (Prophetic traditions) and Islamic history.

After completing his early education under the guidance of his learned father, he moved to Lahore and Sialkot (in present-day Pakistan), both of which at the time were prominent centres of Islamic learning in India. He received advanced training in tafsir (Qur'anic commentary), *Hadith*, *fiqh*, *mantiq* (logic), *falsafah* (philosophy) and *kalam* (theology) under the guidance of eminent scholars. Ahmad was a gifted student who not only possessed a highly retentive memory but also required minimal instruction from his tutors. At the age of seventeen, he returned home after completing his studies and began to teach at his local Islamic seminary.

Soon his name and fame spread throughout Sirhind because of his vast knowledge of Islam. But later he left his native town and moved to Agra, the capital of the Mughal dynasty, where he joined Emperor Akbar's circle of courtiers. He was shocked to see the intellectual weakness and materialistic passions of the ruling elites. When he challenged their un-Islamic ideas and practices, prominent Mughal ministers, such as Abul Fadl and Abul Faid, made life difficult for him, thus forcing him to leave Agra and return to his native Sirhind.

During this period, he married and also began to study Sufism under his father's guidance. As a distinguished Sufi of the *qadiriyah* and *chishtiyah* lineage, his father was thoroughly familiar with the works of outstanding Sufi theoreticians like al-Kalabadhi, al-Suhrawardi and ibn al-Arabi (see chapter 65).

After his father died in 1598 CE, Ahmad left Sirhind to perform the sacred pilgrimage to Makkah. On his way, he met the celebrated Naqshbandi Sufi, Khwajah Baqi Bi'llah, who helped him to progress through all the stages of spiritual experience. Thus, he experienced the spiritual stages such as *fana* ('self-annihilation'), *jam al-jam* ('absolute union'), *farq ba'd al-jam* ('separation after union') and *maqam al-takmil* ('perfect station') much quicker than the Khwajah had expected. As a gifted scholar and Sufi, Ahmad was determined to reach the highest peak of Islamic spirituality so he could distinguish the reality of *tasawwuf* from the chaff of popular Sufism. After Khwajah Baqi Bi'llah died in 1603 CE, he again returned to Sirhind where he devoted the rest of his life to the pursuit of Islamic knowledge, wisdom and spirituality. He also became a powerful champion of traditional Islam in Muslim India.

Ahmad not only experienced all the *maqamat* (stages) of spiritual l experience, but he also classified his experiences into three broad categories. These were the stage of *wahdat al-wujud* ('Unity of Being'); *wahdat al-shuhud* ('Unity of Witnesses')and *ubadiyah* ('Servanthood'). According to him, the vast majority of the Sufis reached the stage of 'self-annihilation' or 'absolute union' but failed to progress to the higher stage of 'separation after union', not to mention the 'perfect station'. This, in his opinion, explained why the majority of Sufis failed to clearly distinguish the *khaliq* (Eternal and infinite Creator) from *makluq* (mortal and finite creatures).

Thereafter, he undertook a thorough and systematic study of Ibn al-Arabi's doctrine of *wahdat al-wujud* (Unity of Being) and disproved it convincingly and comprehensively. According to Ahmad, none of *anbiya Allah* (Allah's Prophet's) preached this doctrine, nor did any of the great Sufis of the past believe in it. The *tawhid* (Oneness of Allah) of the Prophets and the early mystics of Islam, he argued, stipulated that Allah was *Ahad or Wahid* (One, Only and Unique) without any associates: that is to say, the Prophetic *tawhid* clearly distinguished the *khaliq* (creator) from the *makluq* (creation). Allah is the Eternal Lord of the entire universe, while the creation was nothing more than His creatures/servants. By contrast, Ibn al-Arabi's doctrine of *wahdat al-wujud* stated that there was only One Being and that everything existed in it.

Such a concept, according to Ahmad, had no basis whatsoever in the traditional Islamic theological or spiritual worldview. While the tawhid of all the Prophets and the early mystics of Islam made a clear distinction between Allah and His creation – thus affirming the non-duality between the Creator and His creation – Ibn al-Arabi's *tawhid wujudi* only served to remove that important distinction between the Creator and His creatures. Tawhid *wujudi*, therefore, contradicted one of the most fundamental concepts of traditional Islam and as such it must be rejected, he argued.

As a distinguished Sufi thinker and theoretician, he rejected the doctrine of *wahdat al-wujud* on both theoretical as well as experiential grounds. He claimed that he had experienced *farq ba'd al-jam* ('separation after union'), which, in itself was a higher stage of spiritual experience, only revealed to a select few. At this stage it is made clear that Being is not One; rather Allah is different from His creation. Thus highlighting the fact that Allah is Transcendent, while man is a mere mortal and a servant of Allah (abd Allah). The realisation that man is Allah's creature and servant is, according to Ahmad, the highest stage of spiritual experience. He referred to this stage as *ubudiyah* (servanthood). After clarifying the distinction between the Prophetic *tawhid* and *tawhid wujudi*, he went on to formulate his own mystical philosophy which revolved around the concept of *tawhid shuhudi*.

In other words, he believed that Unity of Being, which the Sufis claimed they experienced when they reached the stage of *jam al-jam* ('absolute union'), was merely 'Unity of Witnesses' rather than 'Unity of Being'. To be fair to Ibn al-Arabi, he also affirmed the distinction between Allah and His creatures but, according to Ahmad, this was not clear enough for the average Sufi, hence the controversy over the true meaning and interpretation of tawhid *wujudi*. Most interestingly, all the great *naqshbandiyah* Sufis believed in tawhid *wujudi* but, after Ahmad's stinging critique of *tawhid wujudi*, the majority of India's *naqshbandiyah* Sufis rejected this doctrine in favour of *tawhid shuhudi*.

His efforts to reform Islamic thought and spirituality in the light of the Sunnah (Prophetic traditions) elevated Ahmad to a very high position in the intellectual history of Islam. Just like his great predecessors Abd al-Qadir al-Jilani and al-Suhrawardi, he was a strict follower of the Prophetic Sunnah. Indeed, he never failed to emphasise the significance of following the Prophetic method in one's day-to-day affairs, as well as one's spiritual practices. Both before and during his own lifetime, many practitioners and followers of Sufism attempted to belittle, if not completely sideline the Prophetic sunnah in their search for so-called spiritual illumination. But Ahmad insisted that following the Prophetic method was not an option; rather it was an essential requirement for attaining the peak of Islamic spirituality.

If he was a great scholar and sharp Sufi thinker, then he was an equally great Islamic reformer. At the time, the Mughal Emperor Akbar the Great and his ministers attempted to dilute the fundamental principles and practices of Islam to please the Hindus. During this critical period in the history of Muslim India, Ahmad and his group of followers fought tooth and nail against the misguided Mughal ruler and his courtiers. They prevented them from stripping Islam of its doctrinal, moral and legal foundations. As a religious freethinker, Akbar regularly organised debates and discussions on philosophy, theology and mysticism in his famed *Ibadat Khana* (Hall of Worship). Here he invited prominent Hindu, Buddhist, Jain, Zoroastrian and Christian scholars and engaged them in religious and philosophical debate.

Over time, he developed – with the assistance of his chief advisors, brothers Abul Fadl and Abul Faid – a new religious blend called *din-i-ilahi*. It comprised elements mixed from Islam, Hinduism, Buddhism, Jainism and other religions. This whole project proved to be an utter shambles, thanks largely to Ahmad and his disciples who vigorously opposed this new creed. For his opposition, Shaykh Ahmad was forced to endure considerable personal hardship and suffering. He even spent a period in prison, yet he did not give up his opposition to Akbar's religious beliefs. This won him widespread praise and approval. From this time onwards he became widely recognised as *mujjadid-i alf-i thani* (the Renewer of the Second Millennium of Islam), even if the concept of a millennial reformer does not exist in traditional Islamic thought.

As a great Islamic scholar, prominent Sufi and outstanding reformer, his name and fame spread across the subcontinent even during his lifetime. He trained hundreds of disciples and sent them to different parts of India to preach Islam as well as establish *naqshbandiyah* Sufi lodges. Soon Sufi lodges were founded in all major Indian towns and cities including Delhi, Agra, Lahore, Allahabad, Patna and Saharanpur. His disciples even took his message beyond the borders of India and established *naqshbandiyah* Sufi centres in Afghanistan, Iran and parts of Central Asia. As a prolific writer, he composed more than five hundred letters on different aspects of Islam and Sufism. In these, he clarified the fundamental principles and practices of Islam and also emphasised the virtues and importance of Islamic thought, practices and spirituality for the benefit of scholars and laypeople alike.

He died at the age of sixty and was buried in his native Sirhind. After his death, his religious mission was continued by his four sons. He is widely recognised as one of India's most influential Sufis and Islamic reformers. Shaykh Ahmad Sirhind's religious ideas and thoughts have influenced some of the Muslim world's most prominent Islamic thinkers and reformers including Shah Waliullah and his sons, Shah Muhammad Isma'il (b. 1779-d. 1831 CE), Sayyid Ahmad Barelvi (b. 1786-d. 1831 CE), Sir Muhammad Iqbal (see chapter 96), 'Bediuzzaman' Sa'id Nursi (see chapter 97), Mawlana Muhammad Ilyas (see chapter 99), Mawlana Abul Kalam Azad (b. 1888-d. 1958 CE) and Abul A'la Mawdudi (see chapter 101), among others.

82

Mulla Sadra
(b.1571 - d.1641 CE) /
(b.979 - d.1051 AH)

The encounter between Islam and ancient Greek, Syriac and Persian ideas first took place in the middle of the seventh century, after Muslims defeated Egypt, Syria and Iraq. As a result, *falsafah* (Islamic philosophy) appeared as a distinct intellectual tradition in the Muslim world. This did not happen until the early ninth century when Muslim philosophers like al-Kindi began to write widely on Islamic philosophy. Their writings subsequently inspired other great philosophers like Abu Bakr al-Razi (see chapter 39), al-Farabi (see chapter 41) and Ibn Sina (see chapter 52) to produce their own philosophical works.

Islamic philosophy flourished in the Islamic East until Islamic reformers like Imam al-Ghazali (see chapter 56) and Fakhr al-Din al-Razi (see chapter 63) came in the eleventh and twelfth centuries to launch a blistering intellectual attack against the *falasifah*. In this battle of ideas, the traditionalists emerged victorious, which marked the beginning of the end of philosophical thought in much of the Islamic East. However, in parts of Persia and Muslim India, Islamic philosophy continued to thrive. This was largely due to the efforts of influential Shi'a philosophers like Qutb al-Din al-Shirazi (who lived in the thirteenth and early fourteenth centuries) and Mir Damad

(who lived in the sixteenth and early seventeenth centuries). But it was in Mulla Sadra that Islamic philosophy found a new, fresh momentum and a degree of intellectual rigour and sophistication.

Muhammad ibn Ibrahim al-Qawami al-Shirazi, better known as Mulla Sadra, was born in the Iranian city of Shiraz into a notable Persian family. His father, Ibrahim, worked as a senior civil servant for the local ruler and attained a position of political importance. As the only son in the family, Mulla Sadra was brought up in a comfortable environment surrounded by much wealth and luxury. Although he began his early education at home, Mulla Sadra was known to have been very hardworking and an enthusiastic reader of books. His sharp intellect, coupled with his highly retentive memory, enabled him to learn and retain a large quantity of information with relative ease.

Impressed by his intellectual abilities, his family enrolled him at his local school for a thorough education in Persian, Arabic, Islamic sciences, literature and philosophy. Soon he completed his elementary education. If Shiraz was a famous centre of Islamic learning, then Isfahan, which was the capital of Persia and the commercial heart of the country at the time, was an equally famous centre of learning. This prompted Mulla Sadra to leave his native Shiraz and travel to Isfahan where he pursued advanced training in both the religious and philosophical sciences. He was guided by eminent scholars like Shaykh Baha al-Din al-Amili (b. 1547-d. 1621 CE) and Shaykh Mir Muhammad Baqir Damad (b. 1561-d. 1631 CE), better known as Mir Damad.

As a highly respected authority on Islamic sciences, Baha al-Din became the *shaykh al-Islam* (supreme religious authority) of Safavid Persia, in addition to being a noted mathematician, alchemist and Sufi (Islamic mystic). Mir Damad was one of the most influential philosophers and jurists of his generation. He was thoroughly familiar with the philosophical thoughts of the early Muslim thinkers and also excelled in Shi'a *fiqh* (jurisprudence). Mulla Sadra studied Islamic theological, philosophical and spiritual thought under the instruction of these eminent scholars, before joining the class of Shaykh Mir Findiriski, who was a renowned Sufi and living at the same time. The latter taught him both *mashsha'iyah* (Peripatetic) philosophy and *hikmah* (traditional theosophy), in addition to aspects of Sufi practices.

After completing his advanced education while he was still in his mid-twenties, Mulla Sadra became very enthusiastic about spirituality. This infuriated the conservative *ulama* (religious scholars) in Isfahan who accused him of promoting un-Islamic ideas. When the hostility of the religious scholars became unbearable, he was forced to leave Isfahan and return to Shiraz. But here, too, he became involved in religious disagreement because he chose to defend certain spiritual doctrines which the *ulama* considered to be contrary to accepted beliefs and blameworthy from a traditional Shi'a perspective. Happily, on this occasion, his influential father came to his rescue and protected him from his opponents.

The Shi'a scholars' reaction against his 'unorthodox' interpretation of spirituality convinced him to leave Shiraz and settle in Kahak, on the outskirts of Qom, one of Iran's most famous centres of Shi'a religious learning. During his long stay in Kahak, he led a simple and ascetic lifestyle and devoted much of his time to meditation, spiritual retreat and intellectual activities. Being competent in both the *ulum al-din* (religious sciences) and *ulum al-aqilyah* (philosophical sciences), Mulla Sadra analysed and re-evaluated the religious, philosophical and spiritual ideas of those before him ancestors (especially the Illuminationist philosophy of Suhrawardi (see chapter 64) and the beliefs of Mir Damad and the School of Isfahan to shed new light on Islamic philosophical and metaphysical thought.

His retreat at Kahak enabled him to re-examine the ideas of earlier scholars and develop his own religious, philosophical and metaphysical ideas during this period. Like al-Ghazali's spiritual experience and awakening, he recalled how his mind became infused with the Divine 'intuitive truths' during his retreat. This, he said, energised his body and spirit, and sharpened his intellect so much that he no longer felt depressed or miserable about anything because the Divine *nur* (light) which entered his being from now on had illuminated his path.

After almost a decade in Kahak, Mulla Sadra returned to Shiraz, where he began to lecture on religious sciences and write books on philosophy, spirituality and Shi'a theology. When his name spread throughout Shiraz because of his vast learning, the ruling Safavid elites offered him lucrative government jobs but he politely turned them down. The Safavids came to power in Persia at the beginning of the sixteenth century and being *ithna 'ashari* (Twelver) Shi'as, they made this the official religion of Persia. Under Safavid support, Shi'a religious learning and scholarship began to flourish across Persia. Mulla Sadra lived during the glory days of Safavid rule. It was a time when the ruling leaders competed with each other to build schools and colleges throughout Persia, and in so doing they created a culture of education across the land.

After his name reached the corridors of power, the Safavid ruler Shah Abbas II (b. 1632-d. 1666 CE) reportedly ordered the governor of Fars to build a religious seminary in Shiraz where Mulla Sadra could teach and train a new generation of Shi'a religious scholars. Despite his busy teaching schedule, he found time to author many books including 'The Book of Origin and Return', 'The Divine Witnesses' and 'Demolishing the Idol of Ignorance', not to mention scores of commentaries on the works of Ibn Sina and Suhrawardi.

Although Mulla Sadra wrote about fifty books in total, his most famous and influential work was *al-Hikmat al-Muta'aliyah fi'l Asfar al-Arba'ah* (The Transcendental Wisdom Regarding the Four Journeys). In this book, he provided a comprehensive, but equally fresh and integrated, explanation of Islamic philosophical and metaphysical thought. According to him, philosophy and prophecy are like two sides of the same coin being. They are containers of the same heavenly truth. He believed that revelatory and spiritual approaches to Reality can provide a sound expression of *al-Haqq* (the Truth). In the same way, he argued, a philosophical approach to Reality can also provide fresh light on the Truth.

In Mulla Sadra's opinion, there was no contradiction between *wahy* (revelation), *aql* (reason) and *irfan* (awareness/gnosis). On the contrary, he argued that they were all complementary sources of knowledge which helped to create a clear, correct and comprehensive understanding of the Truth. To prove this point, he traced the history of religion and philosophy from his own time – through the Muslim philosophers, Shi'a Imams and Sufis – all the way back to the ancient Greek philosophers who, he claimed, had received inspiration from Abraham who, in turn, received the Truth directly from Adam.

By developing such an unusual interpretation of philosophical history, he was able to argue that *wahy* (revelation), *hikmat* (philosophy) and *irfan* (awareness) had originated from the same source. Thus, they had to be complementary rather than contradictory.

This paved the way for him to create a blend between Greek philosophy, the gnostic wisdom of the Sufis and the Peripatetic thought of the falasifah, with Shi'a theology. It is this blend which became known as *hikmat al-muta'aliyah* (the transcendental wisdom).

As a remarkable scholar and thinker, Mulla Sadra meticulously surveyed the intellectual history of Islam before thoroughly studying the Greek philosophical tradition. Thereafter, he presented his findings in his book 'The Transcendental Wisdom Regarding the Four Journeys'. Mulla Sadra was heavily influenced by the Peripatetic thought of Ibn Sina; the *ishraqi* (Illuminationist) philosophy of Suhrawardi; the Sufi cosmology of Ibn al-Arabi as well as Shi'a theology. Mulla Sadra accepted Neoplatonic emanationism (the idea that everything always existed and was not created) but rejected Aristotelian philosophy. He also adopted Ibn al-Arabi's concept of nur *muhammadiyah* (the Muhammadan Light) but strongly opposed Ibn Sina's notion of the eternity of the world. Furthermore, he accepted that the Prophet Muhammad was the *khatam al-anbiya* ('Seal of the Prophets'). But, at the same time, he stated that the true meaning of the revelation would not become clear until after the advent of the *mahdi*, the final Shi'a Imam.

Through this, he united philosophical and gnostic thought with Shi'a theology and developed a fresh and unified Islamic worldview. In other words, through his *hikmat al-muta'aliyah* (metaphysical philosophy), Mulla Sadra attempted to harmonise philosophy, *irfan* (gnosticism) and theology to answer some of the most fundamental questions about Allah, His Nature and Attributes, the meaning of life, the purpose of creation and the nature of the resurrection. All of these were surveyed through the lenses of revelation, reason, intuition and experience. In other words, this was a final summary of a whole philosophy. Whether one agrees with all his ideas or not, one cannot fail to admire his sincerity of purpose, vast knowledge and considerable analytical skills and ability.

Despite being a full-time teacher and a great writer, Mulla Sadra found time to train many influential scholars who also became outstanding promoters of philosophy, spirituality and theology in Persia. His most famous students included thinkers like Mulla Fayd Kashani (b. 1598-d. 1680 CE), and al-Lahiji (d. 1662 CE) – both of whom were married to his daughters. In addition to this, Mulla Sadra performed the sacred *hajj* seven times and died in Basrah at the age of seventy, on his way home from completing his seventh pilgrimage.

Today, he is considered to be one of the great Muslim philosophers because of his original contributions to the field of Islamic philosophy. However, other than in Iran and parts of Iraq and India, his ideas and thoughts are not widely known in the Muslim world. Moreover, his works were not translated into Western languages until; as such, his religious, philosophical and spiritual ideas have not received much publicity in the West either.

On the other hand, in Iran, some of the country's most outstanding scholars like, Mulla Ali Nuri (d. 1830 CE), Sayyid Muhammad Husayn Tabataba'i (b. 1904-d. 1981 CE) and Mehdi Ha'iri-Yazdi (b. 1923-d. 1999 CE) and others have acknowledged their great debt to Mulla Sadra. Thanks to some contemporary scholars like Max Horten (b. 1874-d. 1945 CE), Henry Corbin (b. 1903-d. 1978 CE), Fazlur Rahman (b. 1919-d. 1988 CE) and Seyyed Hossein Nasr (b. 1933 CE), his works are now being increasingly spread across Europe and America.

83

Shah Jahan
(b.1592 - d.1666 CE) /
(b.1001 - d.1077 AH)

The Mughal dynasty was founded by Zahir al-Din Babar (Babur) in 1526 CE. It ruled the Indian subcontinent for more than three centuries with great brilliance and benevolence. It was expanded and consolidated by Akbar the Great (see chapter 80) during his long rule of forty-nine years. The Mughal dynasty subsequently became one of the Muslim world's foremost political and military powers, along with the Ottomans and the Safavids. After the death of Akbar, his son Salim (also known as Emperor Jahangir, b. 1569-d. 1627 CE) ascended the throne and attempted to further consolidate Mughal power and authority. However, he encountered many political obstacles and internal challenges. Jahangir may have been a successful ruler, but he was also a pleasure-seeker who surrounded himself with much wealth and luxury. After securing Mughal rule in Bengal, he built some of the most beautiful fountains and gardens ever constructed by a Mughal ruler.

Unlike his father, Jahangir was highly educated and wrote his autobiography, *Tuzuk-i-Jahangir* (Memoirs of Jahangir), which is today considered to be a work of considerable historical significance and literary merit. The fact that Jahangir was more a conqueror of hearts than of land is most evident from the fact that peace and prosperity reigned supreme during his rule. But towards the end of his reign of twenty-two years, he became involved in a serious internal family dispute, sparked off by the question of political succession. The disagreement divided the royal family and severely undermined his political power and authority. Jahangir was eventually succeeded by his son, Shah Jahan, who went on to become one of the Muslim world's most famous and romantic rulers.

Shihab al-Din Muhammad Khurram Sahib-i-Qiran II, better known as Shah Jahan (King of the World), was born during the long and successful rule of his grandfather, Akbar the Great. His birth was considered to be a good omen for the Mughals because, in that same year, Akbar went on to extend Mughal rule in the north of India. Overjoyed at the birth of his third grandson, Akbar named him 'Khurram', meaning 'joy and happiness'. The Mughal astrologers observed the patterns of the stars at the time of Shah Jahan's birth. According to them, they were similar to the constellations observed at the birth of Amir Timur (see chapter 76), the great ancestor of the Mughals, and this was considered to be a good omen for the boy.

Brought up by his father, young Shah Jahan received a thorough education in the languages, arts and religious sciences. Though his father, Jahangir, led a lavish lifestyle and was very fond of wine, Shah Jahan grew up to be a sensible young man who hated alcohol. Such was his dislike of natural materialism and pleasure-seeking that he even criticised his father for his alcohol addiction. Perhaps it was his early Islamic education which safeguarded him from the wayward and un-Islamic practices which existed within the royal family at the time.

In 1611 CE, when Shah Jahan was nineteen, his father married Mihr al-Nisa, popularly known as Nur Jahan (Light of the World), who was the daughter of a Persian immigrant. Being very intelligent, exceptionally beautiful and highly ambitious, she began to exert undue influence on her husband shortly after their marriage. She convinced her husband to appoint her father Mirza Giyath Beg and her brother Asaf Khan to two of the highest political posts in the land. She then married her daughter by her first husband to Jahangir's youngest son, Prince Shahryar, thus further strengthening her position in the Mughal hierarchy.

As Jahangir increasingly became reliant on his dictating wife to carry out his duties and obligations as emperor, Shah Jahan, who at the time lived with the royal family, co-operated closely with Nur Jahan and her brother Asaf Khan (who was the Prime Minister at the time) to discharge the affairs of State. But he co-operated with them on the understanding that he was his father's heir apparent. Not surprisingly, during this period Shah Jahan served his father with much loyalty and distinction including leading several military expeditions against their rivals. Indeed, when he captured the kingdom of Ahmadnagar in 1616 CE, Jahangir was so delighted with his son's achievement that he granted him the royal title of 'Shah Jahan'.

However, Nur Jahan was not very fond of Shah Jahan. She became very jealous of him to the extent that she began to secretly plot against him. Soon after marrying her daughter to Prince Shahryar, she began to exert her political authority and push for her son-in-law to be crowned emperor after her husband's death, even though everyone within the royal family knew that Shah Jahan was Jahangir's nominated heir. This was a dangerous and unique move on the part of Nur Jahan. As an intelligent young man, it did not take Shah Jahan too long to realise what was happening, but he was determined not to be sidelined or pushed aside. Predictably, this sparked off a serious and damaging succession battle within the royal family. Irritated by Nur Jahan's political plots and by his father's apparent inability to restrict her, Shah Jahan eventually revolted against the emperor.

The timing of his rebellion could not have come at a worse time for Emperor Jahangir because, at the same time, the Mughals had also lost the northern province of Qandahar to Shah Abbas, the Safavid ruler of Persia. He was faced with foreign invasion in the Northwest and open rebellion from his son at home, so Jahangir found himself caught between a rock and a hard place. When the news of Shah Jahan's takeover of Bihar and Bengal was relayed to Jahangir, he sent Prince Parvez and Mahabat Khan to go and crush his rebellious son and his supporters. After suffering defeat on the battlefield, Shah Jahan went on the run, only to be reunited with his ill father in 1625 CE. By then, however, considerable loss and damage had already been inflicted on Mughal power and authority.

As for Nur Jahan, the instigator of this whole sorry tale, her hopes of seeing her son-in-law succeed her husband were also shattered.

Indeed, as soon as the news of Jahangir's death was announced, Prince Shahryar took control of the public treasury in Lahore and installed himself as the new Mughal emperor, but Shah Jahan had other ideas. Until that time he was confined to the Deccan region on his father's orders, now he swiftly moved to Agra, the capital of the Mughal dynasty. There he found a powerful supporter and ally in the person of Asaf Khan, his father-in-law and the serving Prime Minister. In the ensuing battle, Shah Jahan's forces, led by Asaf Khan, defeated Shahryar's army, thereby paving the way for Shah Jahan to formally ascend the Mughal throne at the age of thirty-six. After being crowned emperor, Shah Jahan transferred more political power to Asaf Khan, the Prime Minister, while Nur Jahan was dispatched to Lahore, where she eventually died in 1645 CE.

Unlike his father, Shah Jahan was a bold and decisive ruler. He swiftly removed all rivals from his path and secured his power and authority throughout the Mughal Empire. Although he inherited from his father a struggling administration which suffered from much corruption and lack of accountability, he reformed the organisation. This helped him to face the new challenges which the Mughals encountered at the time. Everything went according to plan at the beginning, and the emperor was delighted by the progress he was making.

However, his success and optimism were soon dampened by two early rebellions against his rule. In the first year of his reign, Jujhar Singh, the Bundela chief, instigated an uprising against Shah Jahan, but he was soundly defeated and driven into the mountains by the Mughals. A year later, another powerful uprising was led by Khan Jahan Lodi, who was an Afghan ruler, but the Mughals hunted him from one place to another before inflicting a final defeat on him. During the next two years, Shah Jahan remained busy dealing with the appalling impact of famine in both Deccan and Gujarat.

During this period, he also had to come to terms with the death of his beloved wife, Mumtaz Mahal (meaning Chosen One of the Palace), the daughter of Prime Minister Asaf Khan. Mumtaz was the real love and passion of his life, and her premature death in 1631 CE was a major blow to Shah Jahan. She not only bore him fourteen children, but her death completely changed his outlook on life. Overwhelmed by grief and sadness, his hair turned white, and he began to wear dark spectacles to hide the marks of tears.

As a prolific builder, during his thirty-year reign Shah Jahan constructed some of the subcontinent's most dazzling works of architecture including the Shalimar Gardens near Lahore, the historic *Jami Masjid* (Central Mosque) in Delhi and the elegant *Moti* (pearl) mosque in Agra. He also built two impressive mausoleums. One in memory of his father, Jahangir, and another in remembrance of Asaf Khan, his loyal Prime Minister and father-in-law, both of which are located in Lahore. In addition to this, he built numerous hunting lodges and gardens in Sirhind, Lahore and Srinagar, and authorised the construction of a new city called Shahjahanabad in 1639 CE. This city was completed in 1648 CE and is today known as Old Delhi. Undoubtedly the most dazzling work of architecture ever produced by a Muslim is the world-famous *Taj Mahal* (Crown Palace), which is the mausoleum constructed in memory of his beloved wife, Mumtaz Mahal.

The Taj was designed to symbolise the greatness and lasting nature of his love for Mumtaz. He personally chose the site, located on the banks of the river Yamuna in Agra, and authorised the construction of this immortal building in 1632 CE. Thousands of labourers worked round-the-clock under the supervision of such distinguished Mughal architects as Abd al-Karim Ma'mur Khan, Ustadh Makramat Khan and Ustadh Ahmad Lahori to complete the huge project on time. After many years of careful planning and hard work, the Taj Mahal was eventually completed in 1648 CE. Made entirely from white marble from the quarries of Rajasthan, the edifice was exquisitely decorated with Arabic calligraphy and floral designs. The texts are mainly from the Qur'an – a total of twenty-two passages including fourteen entire *suras* (chapters). More than three and a half centuries after its completion, the Taj Mahal continues to inspire and overwhelm its visitors to this day. It is not only a symbol of everlasting love, today it is also considered to be one of the seven architectural wonders of the world.

As Shah Jahan was a prolific builder. He was also a just and competent ruler who took decisive action against his opponents as and when required including the Hindu Rajputs who were causing havoc within the Mughal territories. After abolishing his father and grandfather's unfair political, economic, legal and religious policies which they authoriszed to win the support and favour of the Hindus at the expense of the Muslims, he restored the faith and confidence of the *ulama* (traditional Islamic scholars) and the Muslim masses in the Mughal authorities. Unlike those before him, he proudly wore a beard, respected and observed Islamic principles and teachings, and outlawed the practice of bowing before the emperor.

Shah Jahan's early Islamic education influenced his thinking and behaviour on these and other similar matters. Some Indian historians have accused him of pursuing anti-Hindu policies; he was far from being a racist or religious bigot. He offered full protection and support to all his Hindu subjects. Indeed, he allowed the Hindus to observe their religious rites and cultural practices without any hindrance whatsoever. Thus, Shah Jahan was a wise, tolerant and just sovereign who ruled his subjects with more understanding and sensitivity than probably any other Mughal ruler. Unlike his grandfather, Akbar, he was not a military conqueror. He was keen to avoid unnecessary military confrontation. He took action only against those who encouraged or supported rebellious activities against the Mughals. To that effect, he sent his son, Aurangzeb (see chapter 84), to confront the Sultanate of Bijapur for their continued opposition to the Mughals.

Being more radical and enthusiastic than his father, Aurangzeb was on the verge of crushing the Sultanate and their militia when Shah Jahan intervened to prevent unnecessary bloodshed – on the condition that the Sultan paid an annual tribute to the Mughals. Perhaps the only unprovoked military campaign he undertook was the attempt to capture Samarqand the land of his legendary ancestor, Amir Timur. In 1646 CE, while the Uzbeks were busy fighting amongst themselves, Shah Jahan organised a large military expedition against the ruler of Balkh, to proceed to Samarqand.

Led by Prince Murad, the expedition returned home having failed to capture Balkh. Shah Jahan then sent a second expedition, led by Aurangzeb, which forced the Uzbeks to retreat and seek assistance from neighbouring Persia. This time, faced with the might of these combined forces, the Mughals suffered a crushing defeat and were forced to return home without having conquered Samarqand. The campaign to conquer the 'Blue Pearl of the Orient' thus proved to be disastrous for the Mughals both financially and militarily.

Their only consolation was that they recaptured Qandahar from the Persians.

His Central Asian shambles aside, Shah Jahan's reign of thirty years was otherwise supremely successful. He strengthened and consolidated Mughal power and authority across the subcontinent, built some of the Muslim world's most beautiful mosques and mausoleums, and spread social harmony and economic prosperity throughout the Mughal Empire. In addition, he promoted understanding, tolerance and dialogue between all his subjects, including Muslims, Hindus, Buddhists, Christians, Jains and others. For this reason, Shah Jahan's reign is today considered to be the 'Golden Age' of Muslim rule in India.

In 1657 CE, he fell seriously ill, which sparked a civil war between his four sons as they each simultaneously laid claim to the Mughal throne. Shah Jahan's last years were therefore the most tragic period of his life. He died at the age of seventy-four and was buried next to his beloved wife, Mumtaz Mahal, inside the immortal Taj Mahal in Agra.

84

Aurangzeb Alamgir (d.1618 - d.1707 CE) / (b.1028 - d.1119 AH)

The Mughal dynasty prevailed for more than three hundred years before the brutal British took control of India. They sent the last Mughal ruler, Bahadur Shah Zafar II into exile in 1858 CE. During the glory days of Mughal rule, India became one of the world's leading political, economic and military powers. It extended from Afghanistan and Kashmir in the north to the Deccan and beyond in the south. Famous Mughal rulers like Akbar (see chapter 80), Jahangir and Shah Jahan (see chapter 83) established an empire which became the envy of the world. Their brilliance rivalled the achievements of the Ottomans, the greatness of the Safavids and the might of the great European nations of the time.

These descendants of Timur, the World Conqueror, ruled a vast stretch of land where people of all faiths, cultures and traditions lived and thrived. It produced some of the world's most famous works of art and architecture, including the immortal Taj Mahal. In so doing they left their permanent marks in the annals of history. The last, equally courageous and most impressive, of all the great Mughal rulers, was Aurangzeb Alamgir.

Muhammad Muhyi al-Din Aurangzeb Alamgir Badshah-i-Ghazi, known as Aurangzeb Alamgir for short, was born in Dahod

(Dohud) in the region of Gujarat during the reign of his grandfather Jahangir (b. 1569-d. 1627 CE). His father, Shah Jahan, who was only twenty-six at the time, served as Minister of the Deccan province. Being very fond of Shah Jahan, Emperor Jahangir trained him in the arts of diplomacy and governance in preparation for political succession. As expected, Shah Jahan became an able political administrator and statesman. However, unlike Jahangir, Shah Jahan hated wine and rejected his father's pleasure-seeking habits and practices. The real love of his life was Mumtaz Mahal (The Chosen One of the Palace), his beloved wife and consort, who bore him fourteen children.

As Shah Jahan's third son, Aurangzeb received the best education money could buy at the time. Moreover, since his father was more sympathetic towards Islam than his grandfather or great-grandfather, young Aurangzeb studied the Qur'an and Islamic sciences during his early years. Unlike his brothers, he excelled in Arabic, Islamic studies, literature and Persian poetry. He became the first person in his family to commit the entire Qur'an to memory. By contrast, his older brother, Dara Shikuh became a religious freethinker who, like his great-grandfather Akbar, engages in religious experimentation. His other brothers, Shah Shuja and Murad Bakhsh remained religiously indifferent and aloof. But Aurangzeb became a devout Muslim who prayed five times a day and refused to engage in any form of un-Islamic activities.

He was barely ten years old when his father ascended the Mughal throne and ruled the country for three decades. During this period, Emperor Shah Jahan became very fond of Aurangzeb because of his intellectual ability, personal piety and excellent courage and bravery. Shah Jahan loved to watch elephant fights. One day he invited all the members of the royal family to come and watch an elephant session. Suddenly an elephant became erratic. Shocked and horrified by the elephant's threatening behaviour, all the members of the royal family fled the scene. The determined Aurangzeb stood his ground as the wild beast came thundering towards him. When the elephant came within his reach, he threw his spear at the beast, hitting it directly on the forehead. In response, the elephant swung its trunk at him, throwing him off his horse, but he leapt up to face the raging beast again. By then, help had arrived for the fourteen-year-old Aurangzeb.

His bravery impressed Shah Jahan who offered him his weight in gold as a reward for his heroism. This incident established his reputation as a gifted and courageous young man. He also became well-known for his mild manners, soft, gentle voice, and sense of humility. Shah Jahan became impressed by his son's good personal qualities and attributes and appointed him commander of the Mughal army. His time with the army proved hugely successful. His military skills and personal bravery on the battlefield soon won him the respect of the Mughal army.

Shah Jahan was delighted with Aurangzeb's progress. He then appointed him to be the Minister of the Deccan region when he was only seventeen. As Shah Shuja, his other son, had failed to make progress in the Deccan, the Emperor was sure that Aurangzeb was the only man who could restore peace and security in that important province. True to form, he came to Deccan and soon established peace and security throughout the province using his carrot-and-stick approach. During this period, he also married the daughter of a noble businessman. A year later his beautiful and talented daughter, Princess Zaib al-Nisa was born. She later became a celebrated poetess and literary figure.

Unhappy with the pomp, glamour and pageantry of the aristocratic lifestyle, Aurangzeb soon lost interest in worldly affairs. He desired to live a simple, quiet and austere lifestyle, guided by the principles and practices of Islam. The uselessness of worldly power, wealth and possessions prompted him to resign as Minister and become a hermit. He was only twenty-four. His decision to abandon all worldly power and possessions in favour of a life devoted entirely to meditation, religiousness and asceticism earned him the anger of his father. He could not understand why the Great Mughal Emperor's son should choose to lead such a lowly lifestyle.

Aurangzeb was stripped of all worldly power and possessions. As a result, he was now able to see what others had failed to realisze, namely the moral corruption of rich and aristocratic life and the decline of social and ethical values in society. The ruling elite ruled over a dishonest and unjust system which threatened to destroy the very foundations of the Mughal dynasty. The rot, he felt, had to be stopped but this could only be done from within. Thus, Aurangzeb decided to return to the royal family and try hard to change the situation from within. With a new sense of mission, he left his hermitage and moved to Agra. His father initially refused to forgive him for apparently disgracing the royal family's name by becoming a hermit. But, eventually, Shah Jahan gave in and appointed him Minister of the province of Gujarat.

As a troublesome province, Gujarat at the time had become a problem on the Mughals' side. However, on his arrival, Aurangzeb swiftly restored peace and order across that province. His achievement delighted Shah Jahan, who then decided to send an expedition to Central Asia to reconquer Samarqand, the ancestral home of the great Mughals. Thus, in 1647 CE, he ordered Aurangzeb to take charge of a force and set out for Central Asia. A determined, resilient and motivated Aurangzeb moved swiftly towards his target, successfully conquering Balkh and Badakhshan on his way. But Samarqand proved to be a different matter altogether. Both the ruler and the people of this historic city put up determined resistance. So the Mughals' dream of capturing Samarqand soon faded away before their eyes. Unable to break down the Uzbek defences, Aurangzeb was forced to pull back and return to Kabul after signing treaties with the ruler of Balkh. This was the Mughals' last effort to extend their political territories through military conquest. Although Shah Jahan's military campaign against the Uzbeks, as well as the Safavids, proved disastrous for the Mughals, Aurangzeb won much praise for his bravery and resilience on the battlefield.

Of his four sons, Shah Jahan was most impressed with Aurangzeb because of his superior intellect and polished military skills, more so than with his other sons. Nonetheless, to prevent rivalry and ill-feeling within the royal family, he made them all Ministers of their own provinces. Despite being a religious freethinker and troublesome individual, Dara Shikuh was put in charge of Multan and Kabul. Shah Shuja was known for his wrongdoings but was still appointed Minister of Bengal. By contrast, Murad Bakhsh was an alcoholic who loved drinking more than anything else in life, but his father made him Minister of Gujarat. The brave, intelligent and accomplished Aurangzeb was re-appointed Chief of the Deccan province.

By putting his four sons in charge of four different provinces, Shah Jahan maintained peace and unity within the royal family until he was taken ill in 1657 CE. The news of his illness prompted his four sons to engage in a lengthy succession battle. And although it was Shah Shuja who initiated the battle for political succession, he failed to win power. After removing his brothers one by one from his path, Aurangzeb became Emperor of the Mughal dynasty at the age of around forty. Soon after becoming Emperor, he initiated a series of reforms which reversed the anti-Islamic policies of his predecessors and instead, he established the *sharia* (Islamic law) in Mughal India.

To Aurangzeb, India was a Muslim country even though people of other faiths and cultures lived and thrived there. But, unlike his predecessors, he was not prepared to give in to the wishes and desires of the Hindus at the expense of the Muslims. He tried to treat all his citizens as fairly as he could. Indeed, his acts of kindness and generosity towards the Hindus were common. For example, on more than one occasion, he donated land for the construction of Hindu temples, including the Kashi Vishwanath Temple in Varanasi.

Nevertheless, he knew that keeping both the Muslims and Hindus happy would not be an easy task. As a devout and practising Muslim, he implemented Islamic principles and practices in India, unlike his predecessors who went out of their way to appease the Hindus. Thus, in Aurangzeb, the long-suffering Indian Muslims found a true champion who proudly wore the badge of Islam and encouraged others to do the same. Contrary to what some Hindu nationalist and Western historians have written about him, Aurangzeb was far from being a racist or religious bigot. Rather he was a man of sound principles who led a simple, honest and austere lifestyle. Unlike his predecessors who surrounded themselves with much wealth and luxury, he shunned pomp and pageantry and lived like a hermit, sleeping on the floor, covered only with tiger skin, and eating little.

Yet, strangely enough, some Hindu and Western historians have tried to harm his character and personality. But Aurangzeb's faith, devotion, good character and sincerity of purpose were beyond criticism. In fact, he cared very little about his appearance and instead wore simple, inexpensive clothes and deliberately avoided jewellery and adornments. The restoration of peace, justice and prosperity across Mughal India was more important to him than satisfying his whims and desires.

Under Aurangzeb's able stewardship, Mughal rule extended from Afghanistan in the north to the Deccan and beyond in the south, pushing the frontiers of Mughal Empire as far as Assam and Bengal, in so doing he transformed the Mughal Empire into one of Asia's leading political and military powers. During his long reign of almost fifty years, he faced many challenges but he fought and subdued them with great determination and success.

As a learned ruler, he became a generous patron of learning, education and philanthropic activities. In his spare time, he used to commit the Qur'an to paper. A copy of the Qur'an written by Aurangzeb has been preserved in the *dar al-uloom* library in Deoband. Also, as a devout Muslim, he avoided all the singers and entertainers who lived at the Mughal royal court, forcing them to move to the courts of Rajasthan and Bengal instead. More importantly, during his reign, Emperor Aurangzeb established a committee of prominent Islamic scholars to review Islamic law and jurisprudence in light of the new problems and challenges which faced the Indian Muslims at the time. In response, the scholars produced the *Al-Fatawa al-Alamgiriyah or Al-Fatawa al-Hindiyah* (The Religious Edicts of Alamgir), a compilation of *Hanafi* jurisprudence, which is today widely considered to be a standard work of reference on the subject.

In addition to this, Aurangzeb constructed the famous Badshahi Mosque in Lahore which is one of the Muslim world's largest and most beautiful mosques. However, unlike his father, Aurangzeb was not a prolific builder. He preferred to lead a simple and ascetic lifestyle devoted to the service of Islam and his subjects, irrespective of their faith, race or background. He set such a high standard of morals, ethics and behaviour that the title of *zinda pir* (the living saint) was awarded to him by his friends and admirers alike. His favourite motto was 'The true great King is the one who makes it the chief business of his life to govern his subjects with equity.'

Emperor Aurangzeb Alamgir died at the ripe old age of around eighty-eight and was buried at the mausoleum of Shaykh Zain al-Haq at Khuldabad, located in the present-day Indian State of Maharashtra. He was succeeded by his sons who, unfortunately, failed to live up to their father's high standards, and the Mughal Empire began to decline irreversibly.

85

Ibn Abd al-Wahhab
(b.1703 - d.1792 CE) /
(b.1115 - d.1207 AH)

The first half of the ninth century was a defining period in Islamic intellectual history. It was during this time that Mu'tazilism (rationalism) gained dominance in the Muslim world under the support of Caliph Harun al-Rashid (see chapter 28), his son al-Ma'mun (see chapter 33) and his successors. These Abbasid rulers became unrelenting champions of Mu'tazilism and enforced this creed as if it were an article of faith. However, the traditionalists, led by the influential Imam Ahmad ibn Hanbal (see chapter 31), strongly opposed this rationalistic belief because they considered it to be both unorthodox and deviated. That is why they opposed and rejected the Mu'tazilite creed and presented the fundamental Islamic principles and practices in the light of the Qur'an and the *Sunnah*.

For more than half a century, the battle between the rationalists and traditionalists raged in and around Baghdad until Caliph Mutawakkil 'ala Allah (b. 822-d. 861 CE) ascended the Abbasid throne and returned to the original religious tradition. Thereafter, the traditionalist approach to Islam – as promoted by Ahmad ibn Hanbal – became a symbol of Islamic orthodoxy in many parts of the Muslim world. Inspired by the thoughts of Ahmad ibn Hanbal, five centuries later, Ibn Taymiyyah (see chapter 72) advocated the superiority of Islamic traditionalism over all other religious methods, including the philosophical and spiritual approaches to Islam. It was Ahmad ibn Hanbal and Ibn Taymiyyah's religious ideas and thoughts which heavily influenced Muhammad ibn Abd al-Wahhab, one of the most influential Islamic scholars and reformers of modern times.

Muhammad ibn Abd al-Wahhab was born into the tribe of Banu Sinan in al-Uyayna (in the Central Arabian region of Najd). His father, Abd al-Wahhab, was a noted Islamic scholar and *qadi* (judge) who specialised in *Hanbali fiqh* (jurisprudence). As the son of a leading local religious figure, young Ibn Abd al-Wahhab developed an instant attraction with the Prophetic norms and practices which his family members followed strictly. Educated at home by his learned father, he committed the entire Qur'an to memory when he was about ten and then pursued studies in *Hadith* (Prophetic traditions) and *Hanbali fiqh*. Thereafter, he travelled extensively in pursuit of higher education, visiting some of the leading centres of Islamic learning and scholarship, including Makkah and Madinah.

During this period, he pursued advanced courses in theology, Prophetic traditions and jurisprudence under the guidance of famous scholars. As a distinguished scholar of *Hanbali* jurisprudence, Abdullah ibn Saif, one of his teachers, lived in Makkah at the time and introduced Ibn Abd al-Wahhab to the religious ideas of Ibn Taymiyyah and his disciples Ibn Qayyim al-Jawziyyah and ibn Kathir. By contrast, both al-Kurdi and al-Sindi, his other teachers, lived in Madinah where they taught Prophetic traditions. Of Indian origin, al-Sindi was attached to an organisation which encouraged the need for reviving the Prophetic sunnah throughout Madinah.

From Madinah, Ibn Abd al-Wahhab moved to Basrah, where he lived for about four years, before settling in Baghdad. Here he married a relatively wealthy lady but following her sudden death, he then travelled to Kurdistan. According to some historians, he then visited parts of Persia, Syria and Egypt, while others say records taken during the time do not mention his journeys to these distant lands. In either case, Ibn Abd al-Wahhab was an intelligent student who excelled in his studies. He was known for his remarkable admiration for the pure complete principles and practices of Islam based on a literalist interpretation of the Qur'an and the Prophetic *Sunnah*. He never hid his displeasure from those who corrupted the fundamental Islamic principles and practices. Thus, during his stay in Basrah, he passionately opposed the popular culture, customs and practices of the locals.

Indeed, the Shi'a population of Basrah came under attack from him because, in his opinion, the Shi'a beliefs and practices had no basis in traditional Islamic scriptural sources, namely the Qur'an and the authentic Prophetic Sunnah. As the majority of Basrah's population was Shi'a, his criticisms sparked a heated and controversial debate in the city. After conducting an extensive study of the Qur'an and the vast literature of Prophetic traditions during his travels in Makkah, Madinah, parts of eastern Arabia and Basrah, he concluded that fundamental Islamic principles and practices were becoming increasingly compromised by people's excessive reliance on spirituality, local traditions, customs and folklore.

As he travelled across Arabia and the neighbouring lands, he observed, to his utter disappointment, how the majority of Muslims had surrendered to the attractions of *shirk* (associationism) and polytheism in their daily lives. This backward move (away from authentic Islam) both shocked and alarmed the young scholar from Najd. He now decided to devote all his time and energy to the revival of authentic Islamic principles and practices as exemplified by the Prophet, his *Sahaba* (companions) and their *tabiun* (successors).

After his return to Najd in around 1735 CE, Ibn Abd al-Wahhab lived in Huraymila with his extended family. Here, too, he witnessed the same carelessness in the observance of Islam as he had witnessed in eastern Arabia and Basrah during his travels there. This only confirmed his suspicion that the dilution of original, pure Islamic teaching was as widespread an experience as he had thought. After the death of his father, he left Huraymila and returned to his native al-Uyayna. Here he also found the locals following popular customs instead of authentic Islamic teachings. In other words, the situation in Arabia was much worse than he had imagined.

According to the noted British Muslim diplomat and Arabist, Harry (Abdullah) St. John Philby (b. 1885-d. 1960 CE), at the time much of Arabia was under the influence of superstitious belief in the effectiveness of charms, offerings and sacrifices, and in the powers of trees, rocks and certain tombs to effect or hasten the satisfaction of normal human desires. This, no doubt, propelled Ibn Abd al-Wahhab to launch his religious mission to stop the erosion of Islam and revive the authentic Islamic teachings as preserved in the Qur'an and Prophetic *Sunnah*. He was thirty-seven when he formally launched his campaign to remove all unIslamic beliefs, customs and practices from Arabia, the birthplace of the Prophet, and restore the pure message of Islam.

However, as soon as he began to criticise the people of Uyayna for their undue affection for spirituality, adoration of saints and the custom of visiting graves and tombs, the locals instantly turned against him. But, supported by the ruler of Uyayna, he continued to preach the message of *tawhid* (Oneness of Divinity) in the face of stiff opposition from the public. When the opposition against him began to gather force, he had no choice but to leave town and move to al-Dar'iyah (on the outskirts of Riyadh). Muhammad ibn Saud (b. 1710-d. 1765 CE), the ruler of the region, promised to support Ibn Abd al-Wahhab in his efforts to remove all forms of superstitious and polytheistic practices (like saint worship and the veneration of holy men and religious shrines) from Arabian society.

In so doing he hoped to refresh the authentic Prophetic practices which, he felt, had been corrupted due to the people's lack of Islamic knowledge, and laziness in the observance of Islam. Like Ibn Taymiyyah and Ibn Qayyim al-Jawziyyah before him, he argued that *ilm al- tawhid* (or knowledge of the Islamic concept of Divinity) was crucial to being a faithful Muslim, and any form of compromise on this fundamental issue was equal to deviation and heresy. According to Ibn Abd al-Wahhab, all forms of worship, adoration and veneration must be directed to Allah, Who alone deserves to be worshipped, praised and glorified.

Like Ahmad ibn Hanbal, Ibn Taymiyyah and Ibn Qayyim al-Jawziyyah, he rejected philosophical and mystical interpretations of the Qur'an and the Prophetic teachings. Indeed, he went out of his way to develop a rigid and literalist understanding of the Qur'an and Prophetic *Sunnah*. Since a literal interpretation of the Islamic concept of tawhid was central to his worldview and religious mission, Ibn Abd al-Wahhab devoted an entire book to explaining this fundamental Islamic belief. His *Kitab al-Tawhid* (The Book of Monotheism) is divided into more than sixty short sections. In it, he provided a comprehensive explanation of the Islamic concept of Divine Unity, based on his literalist reading of the Qur'an and authentic Prophetic traditions.

He was convinced that Muslims had both compromised and deviated from pure Islam. So he urged the public to abandon all unworthy beliefs and practices, and instead concentrate on the Qur'an and authentic Sunnah – like the *salaf al-salih* (the pious predecessors). Ibn Abd al-Wahhab authored several other books like 'The Three Principles and their Evidence' and 'Exhortations of the Shaykh', which is a collection of religious sermons. In these and other similar works, he interpreted *tawhid* in its pure and unchanged form. He believed that his understanding of this fundamental Islamic concept provided a sound basis for a modern Islamic State and society.

With this in mind, in 1744 CE, he and Muhammad ibn Saud formed a political and religious alliance to establish an Islamic State in Arabia. He actively supported Muhammad ibn Saud to unify Arabia under his political leadership. Ibn Saud gave him full freedom to propagate his religious teachings across the country. The alliance between Ibn Abd al-Wahhab and Ibn Saud provided the basis on which the Kingdom of Saudi Arabia was to be founded by Abd al-Aziz ibn Saud (b. 1875-d. 1953 CE) during the early part of the twentieth century. Thus, the al-Saud–al-Shaykh agreement played a pivotal role in the formation of Saudi Arabia as a political and religious entity and defined how Islam was to be interpreted and practised in that country. Indeed, with Ibn Saud's full support and backing, Ibn Abd al-Wahhab developed a literalist interpretation of Islamic theology and jurisprudence. He was a clever political operator so he used the state organisations and systems to implement his interpretation of Islam across all sections of Arabian society.

As a result, he became an immensely powerful religious figure in that country. As a firm believer in the Islamic concept of Divine Unity, he felt the social, political and economic spheres of human activities must also operate under the principles of tawhid. That is why, he went out of his way to integrate the social and political features of the State with his tawhid-centred worldview. Thus, the worship of saints, Sufis and veneration of tombs was outlawed and the failure to conduct the social, political, legal and economic spheres of human work by following the *Sharia* (Divine law)was also considered by Ibn Abd al-Wahhab to be a form of *shirk* (violation of *tawhid*). This, therefore, provided him and his followers with the religious justification for their political and religious alliance with Muhammad ibn Saud.

However, in the subject of fiqh, he was against the *taqlid* (imitation) of *fuqaha* (medieval jurists) like Abu Hanifah, Malik ibn Anas, al-Shafi'i, Ahmad ibn Hanbal and others. Indeed, he considered an uncritical imitation of medieval jurists to be a form of blameworthy and detestable *bida* (religious innovation). Instead, he advocated the use of *ijtihad* (or independent juristic reasoning based on the Qur'an and authentic Prophetic traditions) to address the important issues of his time. As a powerful and appealing religious reformer – and a close friend of Muhammad ibn Saud and his successors – he was able to spread his religious ideas, throughout Arabia during his lifetime. Even after the death of Muhammad ibn Saud, he remained a close supporter of the House of Saud.

This enabled him to further strengthen his alliance with Ibn Saud's descendants; an alliance which continues to influence Saudi politics and approach to Islam to this day. Over time, the Islamic revivalist movement initiated by Ibn Abd al-Wahhab became so powerful that some of the Muslim world's most prominent scholars and reformers, like Muhammad Rashid Rida (b. 1865-d. 1935 CE), Sayyid Ahmad Barelvi (b. 1786-d. 1831 CE), Haji Shari'atullah of Bengal (b. 1781-d. 1840 CE), Shah Muhammad Isma'il (b. 1779-d. 1831 CE), Sir Muhammad Iqbal (see chapter 96), Hasan al-Banna (see chapter 103) and Abul A'la Mawdudi (b. 1903-d. 1979 CE) were, one way or another, influenced by its message.

Another reason why Ibn Abd al-Wahhab has been rated so highly in this book is that his teachings have profoundly influenced Islamic reform movements across the world, mainly due to Saudi Arabia's generous funding of mosques, Islamic schools and free distribution of Islamic literature across the globe. Ibn Abd al-Wahhab died at the ripe old age of eighty-nine and was laid to rest in an unmarked grave according to his instructions.

86

Shah Waliullah
(b.1703 - d.1762 CE) /
(b.1115 - d.1173 AH)

The signs of Islamic political, economic and academic decline became clear for everyone to see during the early years of the eighteenth century. The once-great ruling powers like the Ottomans (1300-1922 CE), Safavids (1501-1722 CE) and the Mughals (1526-1857 CE) faced challenges at home and external threats from foreign powers. Their failure to address the rising political, economic and academic crises which confronted them at the time undermined their political authority at home and made them increasingly vulnerable to the ambitious European colonial powers. They were caught between a rock and a hard place. So the Muslim rulers of the time struggled to maintain their grip on power.

During this chaos and confusion, however, there emerged many remarkable Muslim scholars and reformers who dedicated their lives to the revival of authentic Islamic teachings and practices. They fought courageously to re-energise Islamic culture and society. Though these scholars and reformers were not in a position to organise large armies and initiate military action against the invading foreign powers, they nevertheless managed to defend and champion Islamic values and principles at a critical point in Muslim history. One such remarkable intellectual and reformer was Shah

Waliullah. He emerged to champion Islamic thought, culture and practices at a time when Muslim India was passing through one of the most difficult periods in its history.

Ahmad Waliullah ibn Abd al-Rahim, better known as Shah Waliullah Dihlawi, was born in the Indian district of Muzaffarnagar into a prominent Muslim family of religious scholars and Sufi greats. His father, Shah Abd al-Rahim (b. 1644-d. 1719 CE), was a notable Islamic scholar and practitioner of Sufism. He traced his ancestry back to the Prophet through one of his grandsons. He also considered famous Indian Sufis such as Shaykh Ahmad Sirhindi (see chapter 81), Khwajah Baqi Bi'llah (b. 1564-d. 1603 CE) and Abd al-Haqq Muhaddith Dihlawi (b. 1551-d. 1642 CE) to be his spiritual predecessors. As a respected scholar of Islamic sciences, especially that of *Hanafi* jurisprudence, Shah Abd al-Rahim helped to compile the *al-Fatawa al-Alamgiriyah* (Religious Edicts of Alamgir). This is a famous compilation of *hanafi* jurisprudence which was requested by the great Mughal Emperor Aurangzeb Alamgir (see chapter 84).

Shah Waliullah spent his early years in Muzaffarnagar and then moved to Delhi with his father, where the latter had established *madrasah-i-rahimiyah*, a religious college, in which he taught Islamic sciences. Shah Waliullah therefore grew up in Delhi under the care of his father and committed the entire Qur'an to memory by the age of seven. He then studied Arabic, Persian and traditional Islamic sciences including *tafsir* (Qur'anic commentary), *Hadith* (Prophetic traditions), *fiqh* (jurisprudence) and *mantiq* (logic) at *madrasah-i-rahimiyyah*. After completing his undergraduate studies at fifteen, he married but unfortunately, his wife died a few years later. During this period his father introduced him to Sufism. He received instruction in the *chishtiyah*, *naqshbandiyah* and *qadiriyah* Orders before continuing his higher education in Islamic sciences. In 1719 CE, when Shah Waliullah was only sixteen, his father died and suddenly the full operational responsibilities of *madrasah-vi-rahimiyah* fell on his shoulders. However, he proved to be a competent young man who not only managed the administrative affairs of the college but also started teaching there.

For the next decade, he remained occupied with the administration of the college. In his spare time, he pursued advanced studies and research into the Islamic sciences, philosophy, spirituality, logic, history, traditional medicine and mathematics. During this period, he read widely and expanded his intellectual horizons so he could think in a multi-disciplinary way. Once he was convinced that he had attained intellectual maturity, he then went to Makkah for pilgrimage. He was only twenty-eight at the time. After *hajj*, he stayed in Makkah and Madinah for over a year and engaged in further study and research in the Islamic sciences, especially in *Hadith* and *fiqh* under the guidance of outstanding scholars like al-Kurdi (d. 1732) who taught him hadith and *fiqh*.

Shah Waliullah then received initiation into the *shadhiliyah* Sufi Order, which was widely followed in Egypt and other Arab countries at the time. He also closely observed the social, political, economic and spiritual condition of the Muslims in Arabia. Though he did not meet his contemporary, Abd al-Wahhab (see chapter 85), the famous Arabian Islamic reformer, his stay in Arabia enriched his knowledge of Islam. It enabled him to experience and analyse the condition of Muslims in the heartland of Islam first-hand.

As a sharp thinker and gifted intellectual, Shah Waliullah preferred to analyse and evaluate issues, whether they were religious or otherwise, from different perspectives and in a systematic way. He was also in the habit of relating things to their outcomes, rather than analysing things in isolation from the wider picture. What he saw during his journey in Arabia confirmed his suspicion that the problems which confronted the Muslims in India were not unique. The Muslims of Arabia, as well as other Islamic nations, also suffered from the same difficulty, namely Muslims were concerned and obsessed with the form of Islam at the expense of its substance. He felt the failure of the Muslim scholars and intellectuals to address the new challenges which confronted Islamic societies – both theoretically and practically – helped to create this sorry state of affairs.

He was convinced that the problems which Muslims faced at the time could not be addressed without redeveloping Islamic thought systematically and holistically (focusing on both the material and spiritual spheres of life). Shah Waliullah hoped to develop a fresh and integrated understanding of Islamic traditions in light of his current condition. Not surprisingly, on his return to India, he witnessed the same social and political problems as he had seen in Arabia. Indeed, after the death of Aurangzeb (the last of the great Mughal rulers) in 1707 CE, the Mughal dynasty began to decline rapidly resulting in relentless political rivalry and infighting within the royal family. The decline of Mughal power encouraged many rebel groups like the Marathas, Rajputs, Jats and Sikhs to become active and carry out politically rebellious activities to overthrow the Mughals.

As one Mughal ruler after another tried but failed to reestablish their authority across the empire, their grip on India became increasingly shaky. Though Shah Waliullah was not a royalist in spirit, he nevertheless had no desire to see Mughal rule in India come to an end, not least because the Mughals were Muslims. His ancestors had once served the Mughals with great distinction. But, as a talented scholar and thinker, he could clearly see what others failed to see, namely that the Mughal dynasty was now in deep trouble. There was very little he could do to stop the rot other than directly engage with the public and encourage them to partake in educational, social and religious activities across the country. Despite the political uncertainty and social unrest of the time, he inspired the Muslims to renew their faith and strengthen their commitment to Islam by leading an Islamic lifestyle.

As a learned person rather than a politician, Shah Waliullah devoted the next three decades of his life to writing and researching all aspects of Islam. As a result, he developed a powerful and compelling Islamic intellectual response to the challenges of his time. He lived at a time of profound political, social, economic, cultural and intellectual crises in Mughal India. The invading Europeans began to exert influence on the affairs of the nation, while the ruling Mughal rulers struggled to restore peace and order across the vast empire.

After centuries of Mughal rule, the Indian Muslims now felt threatened by the Hindus from within India and the European colonial powers from outside. As a multi-disciplinary thinker, Shah Waliullah tackled these complex and overlapping social, political, economic, cultural, philosophical and religious issues in more than forty books which he authored in both Arabic and Persian. Just as Shaykh Ahmad Sirhindi claimed to be the *mujaddid* (religious regenerator) of his age, likewise, Shah Waliullah considered himself to be the *mujaddid* of the eighteenth century. After returning from his trip to Arabia, his main *priority* was to return to the original scriptural sources of Islam and analyse them in the context of eighteenth-century Mughal India. He approached his task with great determination and resolve, writing abundantly on a wide range of Islamic disciplines. Thus, he provided Islamic answers to some of the most burning issues of his time.

Some of his well-known books include 'The Divine Explanations', 'Curing the Hearts', *Izalat al-Khafa 'an Khilafat al-Khulafa* (Removal of Ambiguity about the Early Caliphate) and *Hujjat Allah al-Balighah* (Allah's Conclusive Argument). In these and many other books, he presented a systematic analysis of historical, philosophical, theological and spiritual thought. He hoped to harmonise the different strands of Islamic thought to create a unified worldview.

He argued that there existed a common thread across all branches of knowledge. This unified the core structures of human thought, even if the scholars of the past either failed to notice this generic truth or completely overlooked it in their quest for the specific – as opposed to the full picture. This innovative approach to Islamic thought enabled Shah Waliullah to reconcile some of the most complex and controversial theories which existed within Islamic philosophical, theological and mystical circles at the time.

In addition to philosophy, theology and spirituality, he conducted extensive research in Islamic jurisprudence, history, political affairs, cultural development, social morality and ethics. His *Izalat al-Khafa 'an Khilafat al-Khulafa* is a refreshing study of early Islamic social, political and cultural history. Likewise, his commentaries on *al-Muwatta* of Malik ibn Anas (see chapter 24), in both Arabic and Persian, provided a detailed explanation of Islamic religious beliefs, morals and ethical teachings. His treatises on Qur'anic sciences (including *al-Fawuz al-Kabir fi Usul al-Tafsir,* Great Victory of Qur'anic Hermeneutics) are today considered to be some of the best works ever composed by an Indian Muslim in the field of Qur'anic thought and scholarship.

Shah Waliullah was convinced that Islam provided a comprehensive formula and method which combined all aspects of human life (including the spiritual, psychological and biological nature of human relationships), without overlooking the political, economic, cultural and aesthetic dimensions. The integrated concept of life presented by Islam had not only become completely eroded in Muslim India in both theory and practice, but to Shah Waliullah, Indian Muslims had lost touch with the original, pristine sources of Islam. That is why he translated the Qur'an into Persian, despite the opposition of the conservative *ulama* (religious scholars), to make the Qur'an more accessible to the masses.

In addition to this, in his *Hujjat Allah al-Balighah*, which is perhaps his most famous book, he developed a holistic and integrated view of life for the benefit of Indian Muslims. He emphasised the role and importance of *ijtihad* (exercise of individual judgement) in Islamic jurisprudence. He argued that through the exercise of *ijtihad*, the timeless teachings of Islam (from the Qur'an and authentic *Hadith*) could be applied in all times and conditions. As a determined champion of Islamic learning and education, Shah Waliullah supported the view that the Qur'an should be translated into other languages. Thus, his pioneering Persian translation of the Qur'an later inspired his talented sons, Shah Abd al-Qadir (b. 1752-d. 1813 CE) and Shah Rafi al-Din (b. 1749-d. 1817 CE), to produce Urdu translations for the first time in the history of India. In this way, he and his son made the Qur'an accessible to millions of people throughout the subcontinent, Muslims and non-Muslims alike.

At a time when the Indian Muslims became surrounded by nothing but doom and gloom, Shah Waliullah's refreshing and enlightening books lifted their hearts and spirits. His reformist ideas and encyclopaedic knowledge of Islam, coupled with his analytical approach to Islamic principles and practices, influenced generations of prominent Islamic scholars, thinkers and reformers across the subcontinent and elsewhere. These included al-Zabidi (b. 1732-d. 1790 CE), Sir Sayyid Ahmed 'Khan Bahadur', Sayyid Ahmad Barelvi (b. 1786-d. 1831 CE), Shah Isma'il Muhammad (b. 1779-d. 1831 CE), Mawlana Karamat Ali Jaunpuri (b. 1800-d. 1873 CE), Sir Muhammad Iqbal, Muhammad al-Ghazali al-Saqqa (b. 1917-d. 1996 CE), Ubaidullah Sindhi (b. 1872-d. 1944 CE), Abul Kalam Azad (b. 1888-d. 1858 CE), Abul A'la Mawdudi and Abul Hasan Ali Nadwi (b. 1913-d. 1999 CE).

Also, for a long time, his famous *Hujjat Allah al-Balighah* was used as a standard textbook at al-Azhar University, one of the Muslim world's most famous seats of Islamic learning and scholarship. It is now available in English. Shah Waliullah died at the age of fifty-nine and was buried in Meruli, a suburb of Delhi, in India.

87

Uthman Dan Fodio
(b.1754 - d.1817 CE) /
(b.1168 - d.1232 AH)

Islam became integral in many parts of Africa as early as the seventh century. After the Muslim conquest of parts of North Africa during the Caliphates of Umar and Uthman, Islamic rule was reasserted throughout that region during the reign of Mu'awiyah. Thus permanently establishing an Islamic presence in North Africa and the region that the early Muslim historians referred to as *bilad al-Sudan* (the land of Sudan) in Northeast Africa. Before the arrival of Islam on the other side of the continent, the West Africans were animists who worshipped animals and other natural objects and led a largely tribal lifestyle. However, after the spread of Islam, Muslim missionaries and traders moved into West Africa and won the locals over to Islam. Today more than half of Africa's Muslim population happens to live in West Africa where Islam continues to play an influential role in all sectors of society.

Some of Africa's most powerful and lasting Islamic revivalist movements also emerged in West Africa. Inspired by the locals' desire to reassert Islamic morals and values in their societies, these movements played a pivotal role in addressing the challenges which confronted the West African Muslims at the time. Some were led by influential leaders like Sheku Hamada in Mansina

(1815-1821 CE), Segu (1852-1864 CE) and al-Hajj Umar. It was, however, the nineteenth-century *jihad* movement of Shaykh Uthman Dan Fodio in Hausaland which became a great source of inspiration for the West African Muslims.

Uthman ibn Muhammad ibn Uthman ibn Salih, known as Uthman (or Usuman) Dan Fodio for short, was born in the town of Maratta in the Hausa State of Gobir. During his childhood, his family left Maratta and settled in Degel, located close to present-day Sokoto (in modern-day Nigeria). Young Uthman grew up under the care of his parents who ensured that he received a thorough education. As a noted Islamic scholar and a man of letters, Muhammad Fodio, Uthman's father, encouraged his son to continue the family tradition by specialising in traditional Islamic sciences. He was brought up in a strongly Islamic environment. Uthman learned Arabic and memorised the whole Qur'an before he was ten. His ability to learn Islamic knowledge and wisdom with ease prompted his father to encourage him to undertake advanced training in traditional Islamic sciences.

He began by attending the lectures of prominent local scholars like Shaykh Uthman Binduri, Shaykh Muhammad Sambo and Shaykh Jibril ibn Umar, who influenced him the most. A strict adherent of the *Sunnah* (Prophetic norms and traditions), Uthman became a close disciple of Shaykh Jibril who taught him Arabic literature, *tafsir* (Qur'anic commentary), *hadith* (Prophetic traditions), *fiqh* (Islamic jurisprudence), *sira* (life of the Prophet) and *tasawwuf* (Islamic spirituality). Of medium height, light complexion and slim build, Uthman led a simple and austere lifestyle. He was also a charismatic and gifted intellectual who earned his living working as a rope twister. In his spare time, he read widely and wrote poetry in praise of the Prophet. Thanks to his vast learning and spiritual ability, he soon attracted a sizeable following and established his reputation as an up-and-coming religious scholar and leader of his people.

During this period Uthman began to observe his people's current condition and what he saw did not please him at all. He thought the people had drifted away from the pure teachings of Islam, as preserved in the Qur'an and Prophetic *Sunnah* and that they had also fallen under the spell of *jahiliyah* (ignorance) and superstition. Rather than compete with one another in the pursuit of things good and upright, they engaged in blameworthy and detestable activities. In the process, some became actively involved in practices which were clearly against important Islamic principles. They did so without even realising that that was the case. This state of affairs existed in and around Degel while Uthman was a youngster.

To add insult to injury, as *bida* (religious innovation) and self-styled mystical activities increased, the local ruling elites were busy accumulating wealth and property at the expense of the poor and needy. The religious scholars, who were supposed to be the guardians of faith, knowledge and wisdom, had also succumbed to worldly pleasures and luxuries. By failing to address the challenges which confronted their society and provide Islamic answers to the problems of their time, they had effectively abandoned their role as the champions of truth, justice and fair play. When the reality of the situation confronting his people became all too clear for Uthman to see, he was shocked and appalled. Indeed, the troubles of ordinary people – who were forced to experience untold personal suffering and hardship – moved him so much that he decided to do something to change the situation.

While still in his early twenties, Uthman became a prolific writer and speaker. He wrote scores of articles and poems on Islamic topics and delivered public lectures on Islamic beliefs and social practices. He was keen to correct his people's misconceptions about the fundamental principles and practices of Islam. He also offered guidance to them in their social and cultural affairs. As a gifted scholar, Uthman was not only aware of the burning issues of his time, but he was also eager to tackle those issues head-on. The people of Degel responded very positively to his call for educational and socio-cultural reform. Accordingly, he gathered around him a group of young men who subsequently became his devout followers and together they began the task of reforming their society in the image of Islam.

His younger brother, Abdullahi ibn Muhammad, who became a prolific writer and esteemed scholar in his own right, soon joined him in his efforts to change and reform their society. When the reform movement initiated by Uthman became very popular with the locals, the official *ulama* (who were in the pay of the ruling elites) tried to undermine his credentials as a religious scholar and leader. But he never hesitated in his efforts to promote goodness and discourage blameworthy activities (*al amr bi'l ma'ruf wa nahy an'il munkar*). This, according to Uthman, was the mission of all the Divinely inspired Prophets and since the *ulama* were the *warith* (inheritors) of the Prophets, their main task should be to promote goodness and eradicate evil from all sectors of society. However, he felt the *ulama* of his community had abandoned this noble duty by currying favour with the local ruling elites. Although this situation shocked and dismayed him, he was very determined to expand his *da'wah* (Islamic missionary) activities despite the opposition of the local *ulama* and Hausa rulers.

During this period, he wrote prolifically, authoring more than fifty books and essays on a wide range of Islamic topics including beliefs and concepts, moral and ethical teachings, and Islamic spirituality and guidelines for his followers. In addition, he fully explained Islamic rules about women and defined their role in society. His unusually progressive attitude towards women's education and their role and responsibility in society earned him the wrath of the official Hausa *ulama*, who strongly opposed his liberalist stance on this issue. Their opposition and criticism did not stop him. Uthman encouraged the Hausa women to pursue education and engage in literary activities.

The women of his household led the way in this respect. Thus his daughter, Nana Asma'u (b. 1793-d. 1864 CE) became one of the most prominent literary figures of her generation. Uthman was an inspirational leader and a practical thinker. His balanced understanding and interpretation of Islamic principles and practices won over the people of Degel and his reputation spread throughout Hausaland. This prompted the King of Gobir to approach him with gifts of money and expensive presents to win him over to his side. Uthman told him categorically that he was not interested in the wealth or material possessions of this world. His prime objective, he said, was to revive the message of Islam and eradicate political oppression, social inequality and economic injustice from Hausaland.

As the Islamic movement continued to expand rapidly, Uthman's followers began to oppose the oppressive policies of the local rulers. Not surprisingly, the Hausa rulers felt threatened by the growing Islamic movement. This forced them to take action against Uthman's followers, who were now routinely harassed and obstructed by the government officials. When the situation became unbearable, in 1804 CE Uthman ordered his close disciples to do *hijrah* (migration) to Gudu, on the northern outskirts of Gobir but, here too, they were harassed by the local Hausa rulers who decided to drive them out of that area. This prompted Uthman's disciples to pledge allegiance to him as their *imam* (religious leader) and *amir al-mu'minin* (commander of the believers). By doing this, they initiated a mass campaign against all forms of injustice and oppression. The Hausa rulers were determined to wipe out this small Muslim community before they could properly organise themselves, so they attacked them first. This left Uthman and his followers with no option but to fight back.

As news of the declaration of the *jihad* (struggle for Islam) began to spread, Uthman's supporters and sympathisers throughout Hausaland revolted against their cruel and oppressive rulers. An all-out military conflict soon followed in which his forces inflicted a crushing defeat on their enemies and in the process, they captured Gobir (the most powerful State in Hausaland) in 1808 CE. Thus securing a great victory for Islam. During this period of warfare, he lost some of his most trusted and capable disciples on the battlefield. Their tragic loss was deeply felt soon after victory was secured. His followers had gained control of a vast stretch of land which they were suddenly expected to govern and do so without their most able and experienced leaders. This proved a massive challenge for Uthman because he considered himself to be a religious scholar rather than a politician, yet circumstances forced him to assume both political and religious leadership.

After five years of devastating warfare, the entire political, civil and administrative systems of the gGovernment in Hausaland lay in ruins, as did the local economy. He might have won the war, but now his greatest challenge was to win the peace. This task, he knew, would not be an easy one. But, assisted by his brother Abdullahi and his son Muhammad Bello (b. 1781-d. 1837 CE), he formed a *shura* (cosultative) council consisting of some of the leading members of the new Muslim community. Together they tried to reconstruct the political, economic and educational infrastructure throughout Hausaland.

After founding Sokoto, the new capital of Hausaland, Uthman placed his brother Abdullahi and son Muhammad in charge of administering the new Muslim State, and they reported directly to him. He then implemented the *Sharia* (Islamic law) across the land and gradually the political and economic situation in Hausaland began to improve. During this period, he continued to write prolifically, focusing on the problems and challenges which confronted the new Muslim State he had founded. As a result, he developed political guidelines, social and economic policies and religious instructions for the civil servants, administrators and Ministers who were entrusted with the task of serving the public. Uthman spent the last years of his life in Sifawa, situated on the outskirts of Sokoto, where he eventually died at the age of sixty-three, without nominating a successor.

However, his son Muhammad Bello, who was an eminent scholar and accomplished military commander, succeeded his father as *amir* (leader) of the Sokoto Caliphate. Although the Caliphate founded by Uthman endured until the beginning of the twentieth century, the impact of his reformist ideas, thoughts, *jihad* (military campaigns), as well as the legacy of the Sokoto Caliphate, continues to influence the religious practices of the West African Muslims to this day (especially in northern Nigeria).

In total, Uthman wrote more than one hundred books and essays on all aspects of Islam and in so doing he became a powerful champion of Islamic learning and scholarship across West Africa. His younger brother Abdullahi and son Muhammad followed in his footsteps and authored more than eighty books each. Despite being a *Maliki faqih* (jurist) and a Sufi of the *qadiriyah* Order, he found time to read and study the works of other *madhahib* (schools of Islamic law). He also considered the followers of the *tijaniyah* Sufi Order to be his own followers. In short, Uthman was a great Islamic scholar, thinker and one of the most influential Muslim reformers of the nineteenth century.

88

Shamyl of Dagestan (b.1797 - d.1871 CE) / (b.1211 - 1288 d.AH)

The fall of the Soviet Union during the early 1990s brought in a new era in the history of Muslim Central Asia. Historically speaking, the people of this region began to embrace Islam during the Caliphate of Uthman and, as a result, this region became a flourishing centre of Islamic learning, culture and civilisation. Also, during the glory days of Islamic rule, prominent Central Asian cities like Bukhara, Samarqand and Tashkent became thriving centres of business and cultural exchange, positioned within the ancient Silk Road. Thus, Central Asia became a melting pot of different cultures, races and traditions, although the Caucasus later became involved in political unrest and turmoil.

Tough, talented and unusually brave, the people of this region survived the horrors of Mongol invasion in the thirteenth century and resisted the mighty Russian and Soviet military machines for more than a century. Being extremely independent-minded, they resented the Soviet invasion. Indeed, their desire to preserve their Islamic faith, culture and traditions inspired them to resist the imposition of Soviet Marxist-Communist ideology throughout the region. But, following the breakup of the Soviet Union in the 1990s, the Central Asian Muslim countries finally gained their independence,

although the battle for the hearts and minds of the Caucasian people continues to this day. The man who inspired the Caucasian
Muslims to rise and liberate their homeland from Russian control,
and revive their Islamic culture and heritage was none other than
the legendary Muslim warrior and freedom fighter, Imam Shamyl
of Daghestan, the great grandfather of Khabib Nurmagomedoc, the
Ultimate Fighting Championship (UFC) Lightweigth Champion.

He was born in the village of Gimiri in North-eastern Daghestan
into a noble Muslim family. Shamyl's real name was Ali, but he later
became known as Imam Shamyl (Shamil), because it was a popular
local custom to change the names of the newborn to protect them
from evil spirits. As a youngster, Shamyl studied Arabic language,
literature, Islamic sciences and Sufism under the guidance of Mulla
Jamal al-Din, a local teacher and Sufi guide. He also became highly
skilled in one-to-one combat and warfare. It was the custom of the
Caucasian people to provide basic Islamic education to their young
ones before they received training in archery, horse riding and
the use of a dagger. He was brought up and trained in the ancient
Caucasian tradition of valour and heroism. Young Shamyl showed
signs of intelligence and physical ability from the beginning. After
being badly beaten up and bruised by a group of local boys, he
received training in self-defence and became an expert athlete
and fighter.

Known for his religiosity and dedication to Sufi teachings from
an early age, he preferred to perform prayers and engage in other
devotional activities at his local mosque, rather than play games or
take part in recreational activities. The people of Daghestan were
gripped by all sorts of superstitious beliefs and practices. They
hardly ventured outside their homes after dark, but brave Shamyl
had no time for such imaginary fears. He regularly went out at
night, perhaps to prove to his people that no devils were lurking
out there under the cover of darkness.

Like the majority of Daghestanis, he was brave, patient and a
committed Muslim but, unlike them, he was not superstitious or
fatalistic. His unflinching faith in the power and majesty of Allah
left no room for fear of men or evil spirits. In that sense, Shamyl
was a true believer who attained a far superior understanding of
Islam than most of his countrymen, who had come under the spell
of a mystical and superstitious brand of Islam. While he was in his

twenties, he became very fond of elegant Sufi robes, which had to be either black or white in colour. He also grew a long, flowing beard to follow the Prophet of Islam. At the same time, his extraordinary acts of bravery and chivalry earned him something of a reputation in his locality. He was not only a fast runner, but he could also leap over seven-foot-high walls and cut down his opponents from their horses with ease.

As the *naqshbandiyah* Sufi tariqa was one of Central Asia's most widely followed Sufi Orders, Shamyl became a follower and practitioner of this tariqa. Also known to have been a gentle and compassionate young man, he was keen to change and reform his society in the light of the authentic teachings of Islam as propagated by great Sufis like Khwajah Naqshband (see chapter 74) and his disciples. However, given the widespread ignorance and stubbornness of his people – and the continuous rivalry within each tribe which was common in the Caucasus at the time, especially in Daghestan – he knew it would not be an easy task to change and reform his society. But he did not lose heart. He persevered and worked hard to improve his people's condition.

He was aware of his predecessors' attempts to remove superstitious beliefs and practices from their society and unify Daghestan and the neighbouring States to face the challenges which confronted their people. Shamyl also knew it was the petty religious and political differences within his society which represented the main obstacle to unity. Unless such differences were overcome or put aside, he felt it would not be possible to unify and organise his people to put up a united front against their external enemies. Historically the battle for the hearts and minds of the people of Daghestan and the neighbouring States was first started by the Naqshabandi Sufi Mulla Muhammad long before Shamyl's time. After that, his mission was championed by the *ghazi* (warrior) Muhammad ibn Isma'il of Gimiri (known as Ghazi Mulla) and his successor Hamzah Beg (who became the second *imam*, or spiritual leader, of Daghestan and Chechnya).

But it was Shamyl who was destined to bring about wide-ranging social and religious reform in and around Daghestan. In doing so he was to unite his people under his leadership to fight against the Russian invasion. While he was still in his early thirties, Shamyl had gathered around him a small band of followers who recognised him as their religious leader and spiritual guide. Together they travelled across Daghestan and Chechnya to educate their people and unite them under the banner of Islam. Shamyl and his disciples received a favourable reception from the locals, who soon began to learn more about Islam.

This way, Shamyl and his disciples began to exercise considerable influence on their people. Although it is true that the Caucasian people were Muslims who regularly attended mosques, sent their children to their village *maktab* (religious school) and were heavily influenced by the *naqshbandiyah* Sufi tariqa, they nevertheless continued to lead their daily lives by local tribal customs and traditions, which often contradicted fundamental Islamic principles and practices. Shamyl and his small band of followers tried to remove such contradictions by implementing the *Sharia* (Islamic law). Despite being a strict adherent of the *naqshbandiyah* Sufism (which was well known for its ascetic ways and practices), Shamyl married more than once and had an extended family of his own. Indeed, his understanding of Sufism was a balanced one. His quest for spirituality and the requirements of the *Sharia* blended harmoniously – with both being connected and dependent on each other within the view of the Islamic universe. In other words, according to Shamyl, both the *Sharia* (law) and the principle (Sufism) were necessary for leading a balanced Islamic life, even if circumstances beyond his control often forced him to spend most of his time waging war against Russian aggression, rather than leading a normal, ordinary life at home with his family.

As early as 1801 CE, the Russians had conquered Georgia and made their way towards the mountainous region of Daghestan and Chechnya to add these territories to their expanding empire. But as soon as Shamyl and his disciples succeeded in unifying the opposing tribes of the Caucasus under the banner of Islam, the Tsar became alarmed. He considered this to be a major obstacle to his imperialist plans. From past experience, the Russians knew that the Caucasian people were great warriors who came to the battlefield, wearing their Sufi robes, to die rather than live under foreign occupation. If capturing Georgia had been straightforward, then the Russians knew that defeating the brave and valiant Muslims of Daghestan and Chechnya would be a different matter altogether.

To make matters worse, the mountainous terrain, dense forests and the cold, freezing climate of Daghestan and Chechnya would present serious obstacles to the mighty Russian military machine. Since the Muslims knew the terrain well and could potentially keep the Russians engaged in a long and expensive military campaign with no end in sight, the Tsar's forces advanced with much care and caution. By ditching their policy of containment, the Russians effectively declared war against the Muslims of Chechnya and Daghestan. In response, Shamyl and his people united to fight their enemy and defend their motherland. In the battle, the Tsar's vastly superior forces bulldozed village after village, until there was hardly anything left standing in Chechnya. Though the brave but ill-equipped and hopelessly outnumbered Muslims of Chechnya fought courageously, they were easily defeated by the Tsar's superior army. In the end, Ghazi Mulla, the then *imam* of Chechnya and Daghestan, and Shamyl narrowly escaped the massacre in Chechnya and moved to Daghestan to reorganise their forces and continue their resistance against the Russian army.

After Ghazi Mulla died fighting in 1832 CE, Hamzah Beg succeeded him as *imam* of Chechnya and Daghestan. Two years later he was assassinated. Shamyl succeeded him as the political and spiritual leader of the Caucasus. Unlike his predecessors, he implemented the *Sharia* throughout Daghestan and inspired his people to continue resisting Russian aggression. As a brave and talented *mujahid* (warrior), Shamyl personally commanded the battle against the Russian army. Furthermore, during the hajj season in Makkah in 1828, he met Amir Abd al-Qadir (b. 1808-d. 1883 CE) of Algeria. From this meeting, he returned home convinced that he was not fighting a lonely battle. Rather he was engaged in a global battle against imperialism and colonisation because Muslims in other parts of the world were also busy fighting foreign occupation at the time. This strengthened his resolve as he urged his people to continue their armed struggle against Russian attacks.

For the next quarter of a century (that is, from 1834 to 1859 CE), the brave people of Chechnya and Daghestan fought against the mighty Russian war machine under Shamyl's inspirational leadership. During this period, they fought, frustrated and demoralised one of the world's most powerful military forces. They also kept more than three hundred and fifty thousand Russian troops trapped in the Caucasus. Although Shamyl knew he was fighting a losing battle because resisting such a large Russian force indefinitely would be a mission impossible, the fact that they held back such a powerful army for as long as they did was in itself a colossal achievement. If the international community had responded to his appeal for help and support, then the situation might have been rather different.

As it happened, nothing more than sympathy and moral support was forthcoming. This meant the brave people of the Caucasus had no alternative but to continue their struggle against the Russian army on their own. This effectively sealed the fate of Chechen resistance for the time being. To save his struggling people from total annihilation, Shamyl reluctantly agreed to sign a peace treaty with the Tsar, which temporarily brought Chechen resistance to an end. But Shamyl's heroic struggle against the Tsar not only won him international recognition, but he also became famous in the Muslim world and across Europe as the 'lion of Daghestan'.

He sacrificed everything including losing members of his own family and relatives in his battle against Russian oppression. He eventually died in exile at the age of seventy-three and was buried in Madinah (in present-day Saudi Arabia). But the *jihad* (collective struggle) he launched against Russian imperialism continues to this day. His bravery and acts of chivalry and heroism have become major sources of inspiration for the people of Chechnya as they continue to fight for their freedom from Russian occupation.

Of all the great Muslim freedom fighters of the nineteenth century (such as Amir Abd al-Qadir of Algeria, Muhammad ibn Ali al-Sanusi [b. 1787-d. 1859 CE] of Libya and Sayyid Ahmad Barelvi [b. 1786-d. 1831 CE] of India), there is no doubt that it is Shamyl's influence and legacy which has proved to be the most powerful and enduring. He passed away in Madinah and was buried in the cemetery of Baqi.

89

Sir Sayyid Ahmed 'Khan Bahadur' (b.1817 - d.1898 CE) / (b.1232 - d.1316 AH)

The Asian subcontinent has produced some of the Muslim world's most influential rulers, thinkers and reformers. Thus, famous Mughal rulers like Akbar the Great, Shah Jahan and Aurangzeb feature in these books because of their permanent political and cultural contributions. Likewise, influential Muslim thinkers, reformers and politicians of the subcontinent like Shaykh Ahmad Sirhindi, Shah Waliullah, Sir Muhammad Iqbal, Mawlana Muhammad Ilyas, Muhammad Ali Jinnah, Abul A'la Mawdudi and Muhammad Yunus appear because of their wide-ranging contribution to Islamic thought, political leadership, cultural reformation or economic development.

These remarkable and gifted individuals were pioneers in their chosen fields of service and effort. Their skill, courage and dedication – as political leaders, religious thinkers and social and economic reformers – have rightly earned them a special place in the history of the subcontinent. Sir Sayyid Ahmed, an illustrious Indian Muslim educationalist and reformer, also belongs to this select group of inspirational Indian Muslims.

Sayyid Ahmed 'Khan Bahadur', better known as Sir Sayyid, was born in Delhi, the capital of India, during the reign of the Mughal Emperor Akbar Shah II (b. 1760-d. 1837 CE). His ancestors originated from Arabia and settled in Herat (in Afghanistan) before moving to Delhi during the sixteenth century. As loyal Muslims, his family members became passionate supporters of the Mughal ruler Akbar the Great and his successors. The Mughals, in turn, rewarded them handsomely for their unflinching support and loyalty. One of those who attained a well-known position was Khwajah Farid al-Din, the maternal grandfather of Ahmed. He served the Mughals as a Minister of State and developed a good working relationship with the British, who manipulated considerable political and economic power in India at the time.

While Ahmed was a child his religious and pious father, Sayyid Muhammad Muttaqi, embraced Sufism (Islamic spirituality). Thus, he retreated from worldly affairs and became a *zahid* (ascetic). Young Ahmed was therefore raised by his aristocratic maternal grandfather, who ensured he received a thorough education in Arabic, Persian, Urdu and traditional Islamic sciences before learning mathematics and traditional medicine. During his early years, Ahmed became very fond of Persian poetry and studied the Bustan and Gulistan of Shaykh Sa'di (see chapter 70) and the *Diwan* of Hafiz of Shiraz (b. 1315-d. 1390 CE) with great interest and enthusiasm.

But, after the successive deaths of his older brother and father, his whole outlook on life changed. He grew a beard and became a practising Muslim. At the same time, he was forced to look for a job to earn his livelihood. Thus, at the age of nineteen, he secured a job as a record-keeper at the courts in Delhi. Being hardworking, he was quickly promoted to the post of *munsif* (deputy judge) by the British authorities. Thus, he earned a monthly salary of one hundred rupees which was paid to him by the East India Company.

During this period Ahmed became a prolific writer who devoted all his spare time to research and writing. However, his writings failed to capture the imagination of the public. But, in 1846 CE, he published his *Asar us-Sanadid* (Traces of the Great), which was a historical survey of Delhi's monuments. This book established his reputation as a writer and scholar and secured him membership of the Asiatic Society of Bengal. Then, in 1855 CE, he edited and re-published the famous sixteenth-century historical work *Ain-i-Akbari*, which was originally compiled by Emperor Akbar's favourite minister, Abul Fadl ibn Mubarak (b. 1551-d. 1602 CE). Although this book received much praise, Mirza Asadullah Baig Khan 'Ghalib' (b. 1797-d. 1869 CE), a great Urdu poet who lived at the same time as Ahmed, wrote a critical review of the book and did not rate it highly.

According to Ghalib, it was inappropriate to focus on past glories at a time when the current condition of Indian Muslims was deteriorating rapidly, especially in the face of British political and military onslaught. Instead, he urged Ahmed to focus more on the social and political challenges which confronted the Indian Muslims at the time. Following the horrific events of 1857 CE, known as the Indian Mutiny, which led to the widespread oppression of Muslims by the British army as well as the expulsion of the last Mughal ruler, Bahadur Shah Zafar II (b. 1775-d. 1862 CE), from India, more than three centuries of Mughal rule abruptly ended. A year later, Queen Victoria was proclaimed Empress of India.

These events prompted Ahmed to review the new social and political situation in India and fight for the rights of Indian Muslims. Indeed, shocked by the political disturbances of the time, he initially decided to leave India and settle in Egypt. But soon he changed his mind and instead decided to work with his fellow Muslims to improve their social, political, economic and cultural conditions. As a deep thinker and persuasive speaker, Ahmed knew the political situation in India had changed irreversibly and as such it was in the interest of the Indian Muslims to proactively engage with the new rulers of their country to protect their interests. In the circumstances, he felt opposing the British would be both futile and suicidal for the future of Indian Muslims. Thus, he decided to cooperate with the British authorities.

Being an intelligent politician, he had no desire to see the Indian Muslims become second-class citizens in their own country. He therefore declared his loyalty to the Crown and this, of course, endeared him to the ruling British elites. In fact, he played a central role in improving the Indian Muslims' relationship with the British authorities who, in turn, called him one of their most 'loyal Mohammedans'. Thereafter, the British rulers regularly sought his advice on all important matters relating to the Indian Muslims. So, for example, when he analysed and identified the root causes of the 1857 CE rebellion in his report entitled *Asbab-i-Baghawat-i-Hind*

(The Causes of the Indian Mutiny), the British elites accepted his criticism of the British army and how the rebellion had been handled. Many of his recommendations for change were accepted and implemented by the ruling elite, to facilitate better communication between the rulers and the ruled.

Thanks to Ahmed's cooperation with the Raj and close contact with its leading figures, his attitude towards the British, their culture and way of life began to change for the better. The more he interacted with his British friends and acquaintances, the more educated, cultured and loyal he found them to be. In comparison, the majority of his fellow countrymen were too busy fighting each other and engaging in both tribal rivalry and religious hair-splitting. However, as a devout Muslim and a patriotic Indian, he was determined to improve the social, cultural and educational conditions of his countrymen, especially those of the Indian Muslims. He was prepared to utilise the relevant features of British culture and education for this purpose.

He was convinced that a thorough reformation of Indian Muslim society was the key to improving the Indian Muslims' current condition. So he became a powerful voice for educational and cultural reform across the country. He argued that there was no contradiction between modern science and Islamic teachings. He also urged the Indian Muslims to study the Qur'an and the life of the Prophet Muhammad in a unified and holistic way. The Indian Muslims, he felt, had nothing to fear from modern Western science and educational philosophy. Rather, the pursuit of science and education was the key to understanding Islam and its role in the modern world. Moreover, he urged the Indian Muslims to remain loyal to the Crown and strive hard to improve their social and economic situation by educating themselves and engaging in business and trade.

During this period, his educational thinking and reformist ideas were profoundly influenced by another pioneering, but often overlooked, Indian Muslim scholar and reformer of the nineteenth century. Although Nawab Abd al-Latif 'Khan Bahadur' (b. 1828-d. 1893 CE) was ten years younger than Ahmed, however, he was at least ten years ahead of his senior contemporary. He had been urging the Indian Muslims to embrace English education at least since 1852 CE and his efforts eventually concluded in the transformation of the Hindu College into Presidency College and the establishment of the Mahomedan Literary Society of Calcutta.

This prompted Ahmed to visit Calcutta where Abd al-Latif invited him to deliver a lecture at the sixth meeting of the Mahomedan Literary Society on 6 October 1863 CE. Inspired by Abd al-Latif's fresh ideas and thoughts, as well as the various activities of the Literary Society, soon after his return to Ghazipur, Ahmed established his Scientific Society. The purpose of the new Society was to translate high-quality, modern Western philosophical and scientific literature into Urdu to make the treasures of modern science, philosophy and mathematics accessible to the Indian Muslims.

However, following his move to Aligarh, and subsequent visit to England in 1869-1870 CE, Ahmed conducted a detailed study of the British educational system and its method. As a result, he developed the idea of establishing a college where the traditional Islamic sciences would be taught in parallel with modern scientific and literary subjects. During his stay in England, he became profoundly impressed by the scientific and technological achievements of the Western world. He hoped that his college would inspire the Indian Muslims to revive the Islamic intellectual and cultural heritage.

While in England he also found time to author his book 'A Series of Essays on the Life of Muhammad' (1870 CE) wherein he refuted the charges levelled against the Prophet of Islam by his European detractors like Sir William Muir. As a proud Indian Muslim, he was not prepared to let the Orientalists have a field day against the honoured Prophet. The publication of this book also proved that he was not a blind imitator of all things Western. On the contrary, he showed himself to be a very intelligent and sharp champion of Islam and its Prophet.

After his return from England, he enlisted help from several prominent British officials and together they laid the foundations of the Muhammadan Anglo-Oriental College (MAO) in 1875 CE, known in Urdu as *Madrasat-ul Uloom Musalmanan-i-Hind*. It was patronised by the British authorities and supported by a group of eminent Indian Muslims. This college offered degree courses in science, arts, law and Islamic sciences.

Prominent British academics like Theodore Beck, Theodore Morison, and Sir Thomas W. Arnold as well as celebrated Islamic scholars like Allama Shibli Nu'mani were recruited to teach at this college. Now known as Aligarh Muslim University, this famous institution of higher education has produced generations of renowned Indian Muslims including Maulvi Abdul Haq, Sir Ziauddin Ahmad, Muhammad Ali Jauhar, Liaquat Ali Khan, Dr Syud Hossain and Zakir Husayn among others.

Ahmed's efforts to reform the social, cultural and educational condition of the Indian Muslims initially received a lukewarm response from his countrymen. But after he had developed a fresh interpretation of Islamic scriptural sources in the light of modern Western scientific and philosophical thought, the conservative *ulama* (religious scholars) became a thorn in his side. Since the Indian *ulama* thought he was seeking to dilute and undermine the fundamental principles and practices of Islam under the mask of modernisation and progress. They branded him a religious innovator. However, this charge was only partially justified. Although his desire to improve the condition of the Indian Muslims was both genuine and sincere, the *ulama* were right to question his reformist approach to Islam.

Heavily influenced by nineteenth-century European philosophical and scientific thought, Ahmed attempted to reconcile religion and science, as if Islam and scientific thought were somehow incompatible. Since he considered nature to be a creation of Allah and the Qur'an as His final revelation, he argued that the *ulum al-jadid* (modern sciences) and the *wahy* (Divine revelation) were complementary rather than contradictory. To prove his point, he interpreted the Qur'an and the *Hadith* (Prophetic tradition) from a philosophical and scientific perspective. And in so doing he pushed aside away all the miraculous events mentioned in the Qur'an. For example, he considered the story about the elephants in *Surat al-Fil* to be either a natural phenomenon or the manifestation of human energy, rather than an act of Divine miracle. Given his ultra-rationalistic approach to the Qur'an, it is not surprising that the ulama severely criticised him for his neo-Mu'tazilite approach to Islamic scriptural sources.

However, the *ulama's* opposition to his social and cultural reforms was unjustified. In other words, Ahmed was right to urge the 'ulama to face reality and provide Islamic answers to the challenges posed by Western modernity. Even Jamal al-Din 'al-Afghani' (see chapter 90) – who was very critical of Ahmed for his rationalistic approach to the Qur'an and wholehearted political loyalty to the Crown – thought that Muslims had to change and reform their social, cultural and educational conditions if they were to liberate their lands from foreign occupation and revive their Islamic heritage.

A pioneer of Urdu prose, Ahmed not only became a prolific writer on religious, educational and cultural topics but also founded a number of important educational institutions. Moreover, he published two periodicals, namely Aligarh Institute Gazette and *Tahdhib al-Akhlaq* (The Muslim Social Reformer), wherein he published articles on all the pressing issues of his day. These were later collected and published under the title of *Maqalat-i Sir Sayyid* (Articles of Sir Sayyid). During the 1860s he also wrote a commentary on the Bible, while his incomplete Qur'anic commentary was later published in seven volumes. In short, Ahmed's wide-ranging political, social, cultural and educational activities won him widespread acclaim from his fellow countrymen, Muslims and Hindus alike.

In recognition of his outstanding services to his people, he was knighted by the British government in 1888 CE. His religious ideas and thoughts, coupled with his educational contribution in the form of Aligarh Muslim University, have continued to exert a considerable influence on the Muslims of the subcontinent to this day. Additionally, his reformist ideas have influenced scores of famous Muslim scholars, thinkers and writers like Altaf Husayn 'Hali', Shibli Nu'mani, Sir Muhammad Iqbal (see chapter 96), Shawkat and Muhammad Ali, Sayyid Sulayman Nadwi, Abul Kalam Azad and Ghulam Ahmad Parvez. He died at the age of eighty and was buried in Aligarh. The Urdu poet 'Hali', who was a celebrated writer and a fervent supporter of Ahmed, later wrote a voluminous but eulogistic biography of this great Muslim scholar and reformer under the title of *Hayat-i-Javid* (The Eternal Life).

90

Jamal al-Din 'al-Afghani' (b.1838 - d.1897 CE) / (b.1254 - d.1315 AH)

The decline of powerful Muslim dynasties like the Abbasids (750-1258 CE), Seljuks (1037-1194 CE), Ghaznavids (977-1186 CE), Ottomans (1300-1922 CE), Mughals (1526-1857 CE) and the Safavids (1501-1722 CE) paved the way for the Europeans to emerge onto the world stage after centuries of political corruption, economic depression and cultural backwardness, and flexing their muscles. Led by the Portuguese, Dutch, French and British, the leading European nations eventually made their way into the heart of the Muslim world during the eighteenth and nineteenth centuries. They then colonised a large part of the Muslim world. The colonisation and division of the Muslim world at the hands of the European imperial powers not only represented a major blow to Islamic political unity and solidarity but also inspired scores of influential Muslim scholars, thinkers and reformers to reawaken the Muslim world from its sleep. Jamal al-Din 'al-Afghani' was arguably the most charismatic and influential of them all.

Sayyid Muhammad ibn Safdar, better known as Jamal al-Din 'al-Afghani', was born into a noble Muslim family which traced its ancestry to the Prophet of Islam, through his grandson al-Husayn (see chapter 13). Despite being a high-profile Muslim reformer, much of his early life is hidden in mystery. He claimed to have been born in Afghanistan, but well-known historians like Albert Hourani (b. 1915-d. 1993 CE) and Nikki R. Keddie (b. 1930 CE) have challenged this. They argue that he was born in a village close to Hamadan in Persia and was therefore of Iranian origin – even though he has become popularly known as 'al-Afghani'. He was taught initially by his learned father and later at religious seminaries, young al-Afghani studied Arabic, Persian and traditional Islamic sciences during his early years.

As a bright child who was blessed with a sharp intellect and powerful memory, it did not take him long to become thoroughly familiar with the Qu'ran, *Hadith* (Prophetic traditions), *fiqh* (Islamic jurisprudence) especially *Hanafi fiqh*, and other religious sciences. He was barely eighteen when he successfully completed advanced courses in Arabic, Persian, Islamic jurisprudence, and philosophy and history. Such was his eagerness to learn that he later gained expertise in aspects of medicine, mathematics, chemistry and other physical sciences.

After completing his formal education, al-Afghani said farewell to his family and set out for India, to pursue higher education and possibly also to go to Makkah to perform the sacred pilgrimage. On his arrival in India, in 1856 CE, he toured the country for a year and witnessed the first rebellion against British rule. This incident marked the beginning of the Indian liberation movement and left a deep impression on young al-Afghani's mind. A year later, he left India for Makkah and completed the sacred *hajj*. He then returned to Afghanistan to work in the government of the Afghan ruler, Dost Muhammad Khan (b. 1793-d. 1863 CE). Al-Afghani was known for his scholarship and electrifying oratory skills. He served Dost Muhammad Khan with loyalty and dedication and even accompanied him during his military campaign to recover Herat from the Persians. Following Dost Muhammad Khan's sudden death in 1863 CE, his son, Sher Ali Khan (b. 1825-d. 1879 CE), succeeded him, but before he could consolidate his grip on power civil war broke out within the ruling family. During this conflict, al-Afghani fell out with some members of the royal family, and he was forced to flee for his life.

Though he left Afghanistan with the intention of going to Makkah to perform another pilgrimage, he soon changed his plans and returned to India for a second time. Following the unsuccessful independence war of 1857 CE, the British took full political and military control of India. Thus, on his arrival in India in 1869 CE, the British initially allowed him to move around freely in the country. But, as the failed mutiny of 1857 CE was a disturbing and frightening experience for the British, they closely monitored the activities of everyone who was associated with the Indian freedom movement. As a loyal Muslim and a prominent scholar and political activist, the British authorities monitored al-Afghani's activities especially closely. Soon they came to view him as a potential troublemaker who, given the opportunity, could stir up political unrest and agitation against their rule in India.

The British authorities were keen to see the back of al-Afghani. They granted him a pass to board a British vessel bound for Egypt. On his arrival in Cairo, he went straight to al-Azhar University, the ancient seat of Islamic learning and scholarship, and within weeks of his arrival, he gathered around him a large following from the teachers and students of the university. Here he delivered regular lectures on all aspects of Islam, philosophy, history and politics. His knowledge, resourcefulness, charisma and electrifying public speaking skills created a huge stir at al-Azhar. During his short stay in Cairo, al-Afghani left a deep impression on all the scholars, teachers and students he met at al-Azhar.

From Cairo, he proceeded to Istanbul, the political capital of the Ottoman Empire, in 1870 CE. As in Cairo, here in Istanbul, he rapidly became a popular figure, thanks to his vast education and regular lectures on Islam, politics and philosophy. After his name and fame spread across Istanbul, he was appointed a member of the Ottoman Educational Council. He was invited to deliver regular lectures at the famous Aya Sofia (Hagia Sophia) and other mosques across Istanbul. Al-Afghani's inspiring lectures moved his audiences wherever he went. Later, when he was invited to deliver a lecture at the Dar al-Funun (department of theology) in the presence of leading politicians, intellectuals and literary figures. However, Hasan Fahmi Efendi, the existing *shaykh al-islam* of the Ottoman State, raised objections against his rationalistic interpretation of the Islamic concept of Prophecy.

In this lecture, al-Afghani argued that Prophecy was more than a spiritual gift. Prophecy had its social and political dimensions too.

Al-Afghani argued that if it was understood properly and translated into practice it had the potential to transform dull and dormant Islamic societies into active and vibrant societies. The *shaykh al-islam* became irritated by his social and political interpretation of the Islamic concept of Prophecy. He also accused him of misinterpreting Islamic principles and practices to create a revolutionary brand of Islam. When Hasan Fahmi's criticisms against al-Afghani intensified, the latter was forced to leave Istanbul and return to Cairo, where he hoped to receive a more sympathetic hearing.

As expected, in Cairo he received a warm welcome from both the Egyptian authorities and academics alike. He was offered a generous salary by the Egyptian Government to teach at al-Azhar. He began to deliver regular lectures on Islamic theology, jurisprudence, philosophy and political science. His informative speeches on all aspects of Islam instantly won him much praise at the university. During this period, he also gathered around him a small group of disciples, which included the influential Islamic thinker and reformer Muhammad Abduh (see chapter 92).

Moreover, having travelled extensively across the Muslim world, al-Afghani witnessed first-hand how the Muslim world had been dominated by foreign powers. To his shock, he then noticed how the public had been kept occupied with only 'spiritual' or 'other-worldly' activities by the traditional *ulama* (religious scholars) at the order of the colonial powers. This prompted him to highlight and emphasise the importance of the political and social dimensions of Islam. He therefore urged the Egyptian Muslim intellectuals to engage in political and social activism to liberate their land from British control. His powerful and daring call for Islamic unity in the face of European colonisation and suppression of the Muslim world was not only welcomed by his students and disciples at al-Azhar but also inspired and incited the masses on the streets of Cairo.

As expected, his message of Islamic unity soon began to ring alarm bells within the highest levels of the Egyptian government, wherein the British elites exercised considerable political and economic power. He was accused of spreading anti-British propaganda. The Egyptian ruler, Muhammad Pasha (b. 1852-d. 1892 CE), demanded that al-Afghani leave the country instantly. In 1879 CE, at the age of forty-one, he was forced to leave Egypt for India. But his eight-year stay in Egypt was an important period of his life because during his time there he managed to successfully spread his progressive and revolutionary ideas across that country. After his departure, his disciples took up the cause of Islamic unity and solidarity and called on the Arabs in general, and the Egyptians in particular, to respond to the powerful call for the unity of Muslims (Pan-Islamism).

In India, al-Afghani settled in Hyderabad where, along with Nawab Yar Jung (b. 1871-d. 1925 CE), he became the co-founder of the Osmania University. It became one of the first institutions of higher education in the country. During this period, he also authored an essay under the title of 'Refutation of the Materialists'. Originally written in Persian and later translated into Arabic by his disciple Muhammad Abduh, this book launched a brutal intellectual assault on the materialistic philosophy of the time. It also severely criticised Sir Sayyid Ahmed 'Khan Bahadur' (see chapter 89) for seeking to strip Islam of its metaphysical dimension to make it compatible with Western secular and materialistic philosophies.

According to Wilfrid Blunt (b. 1840-d. 1922 CE), from India, he went to America and stayed there for a few months before proceeding to London, where he became a good friend of Lord Salisbury (1830-d. 1903 CE), former British Foreign Secretary. From London, he moved to Paris in 1883 CE, and there he and Muhammad Abduh jointly published the famous journal *al-urwa al-wuthqa* (The Unbreakable Bond). Through this journal, they sought to awaken the Muslim world from its deep sleep. Both the master and student wrote inspiring articles to remind Muslims of their duties to Allah and their fellow brethren. They urged their Muslim readers to unite under the banner of Islam and liberate the Muslim world from foreign political and military occupation. The journal was considered to be highly inflammatory and was banned by the British authorities in Egypt and India. Although the journal soon ended, it nevertheless had considerable influence in many Muslim countries, especially in the Arab world.

From Paris, al-Afghani moved to Russia where he lived for four years and helped the Russian Muslims publish the Qur'an there for the first time. He was now considered to be one of the Muslim world's most influential advocates of Islamic unity and solidarity. Later, in 1889 CE, he met Nasir al-Din Shah Qajar (b. 1831-d. 1896 CE), the then Shah of Iran, in Munich in Germany. The Shah persuaded al-Afghani to accompany him to Persia, where al-Afghani enjoyed the patronage of the Shah until political conspiracy forced him to leave. At the invitation of the Ottoman Sultan Abd al-Hamid II (b. 1842-d. 1918 CE), he then moved to Istanbul in 1892 CE where the Sultan offered him a generous monthly salary and a furnished cottage. He spent the last five years of his life in Istanbul, although the Sultan's jealous courtiers repeatedly tried to accuse him of political plots. As an intellectual and a reformer, al-Afghani travelled from one end of the Muslim world to the other to raise the Muslims' awareness of their faith and culture, and to champion the cause of Islamic unity and solidarity. He had a high vision for the Muslim world and worked tirelessly to translate his vision into reality. He wanted to revive the *ummah* (global Islamic community) from both political and intellectual stagnation.

Indeed, as the 'father of modern pan-Islamism', al-Afghani was responsible for initiating one of the most powerful political movements of modern times. Though, it is true that he did not achieve his political objectives during his lifetime, the sparks he lit later spread across the Muslim world like a raging flame, as the European colonial powers were, one by one, driven out from the Muslim world. Al-Afghani was not only a political revolutionary, but he was also an outstanding intellectual and a linguist who knew more than seven languages including Arabic, Persian, French, English and Russian.

As an avid reader of Arabic and Persian literature, he was thoroughly familiar with both traditional and modern Islamic thought and scholarship. Being too occupied with political and social activism, he had no time to marry and therefore remained a confirmed bachelor all his life. His political and religious thoughts greatly influenced some of the Muslim world's foremost scholars, thinkers and reformers, including Muhammad Abduh, Muhammad Rashid Rida (b. 1865-d. 1935 CE), Sir Muhammad Iqbal (see chapter 96), and Muhammad al-Tahir ibn Ashur (b. 1879-d. 1973 CE), among others. The determined al-Afghani died at the age of fifty-nine and was laid to rest in Istanbul, Turkey. Then, on 2nd January 1945 CE, his remains were transferred to Afghanistan and reburied at Aliabad, located on the outskirts of Kabul.

91

The Mahdi of Sudan (b.1844 - d.1885 CE) / (b.1260 - d.1303 AH)

Sudan is an enormous African country. It borders eight other countries, is about half the size of Europe, and links the Arab world with the continent of Africa. Its landscape includes deserts, savannahs and forests. The River Nile and its tributaries have also been a key feature in Sudan's political and economic development, making it an attractive target for foreign colonial powers. Due to its geostrategic importance, the forces of Muhammad Ali Pasha (b. 1769-d. 1849 CE), the Ottoman viceroy of Egypt, established their political and economic control over Sudan during the 1870s. It is divided into two large regions, namely the north and south. The former region is inhabited primarily by Arabic-speaking Muslims and Khartoum, the capital of Sudan, is located in this part of the country.

By contrast, southern Sudan is inhabited mainly by tribal people, some of whom are either converts to Christianity or Islam, while the majority are pagans who speak Sudanic languages and observe traditional African customs and traditions. However, as a strategically important country, Sudan became the centre of a global power struggle between the Ottomans, the Egyptians and the British during the nineteenth century. They fought each other to establish their political and economic control in that country.

In such prevailing political chaos and social and economic uncertainty, the towering figure of the Mahdi emerged to free Sudan from the grip of the colonial and imperial powers and return theat country to its people.

Muhammad Ahmad ibn Abdullah, better known as the Mahdi of Sudan, was born on Labab Island, located in the region of Dongola in northern Sudan. His family claimed to be the descendants of the Prophet through his grandson Hasan, the eldest son of Caliph Ali (see chapter 3). His father, Abdullah Fahl, was a successful businessman who earned his living building and supplying wooden boats to local merchants, traders and fishermen. When Muhammad Ahmad was only five, his family was forced to leave Dongola due to an acute shortage of timber in that region. They settled in Karari, near Omdurman and Khartoum, where timber was readily available at the time.

Following in the footsteps of their father, Muhammad Ahmad's brothers also became carpenters. They provided much-needed support for their father to meet the growing demand for timber boats in that locality. Since both his parents were practising Muslims, Muhammad Ahmad grew up in a religious atmosphere.

Keen to provide a sound religious education for his son, Abdullah Fahl enrolled him at his local village school. But, after his father's death, his oldest brother assumed responsibility for the entire family. He encouraged Muhammad Ahmad to continue his studies. As a gifted student, he not only learned Arabic but also committed the entire Qur'an to memory before he was ten. Impressed by his educational achievements, both his teachers and brothers encouraged him to continue his education. For the next seven years, he pursued further and higher education in Islamic sciences, including *kalam* (theology), *tafsir* (Qur'anic commentary), *fiqh* (Islamic jurisprudence) and *Hadith* (Prophetic traditions) under the guidance of outstanding scholars.

During this period Muhammad Ahmad became thoroughly familiar with the writings of classical Islamic scholars like al-Bukhari (see chapter 13), Ahmad ibn Hanbal (see chapter 20) and al-Shafi'i (see chapter 18) and the theological and other works of Ibn Taymiyyah (see chapter 26) and his prominent students like Ibn Qayyim al-Jawziyyah and ibn Kathir. He was also familiar with the spiritual writings of popular Sufis like Ibn al-Arabi (see chapter 59), Ahmad ibn Idris (b. 1750-d. 1837 CE) and al-Sanusi (b. 1787-d. 1859 CE). His literalist theological and juridical training, along with a thorough familiarisation with Islamic spiritual thought and philosophy, later helped him to create a powerful synthesis between Islamic law and spirituality to develop a balanced Islamic character and society.

After completing his formal studies at the age of seventeen, he was initiated into the *sammaniyah* Sufi Order by its influential practitioner, Shaykh Muhammad Sharif Nur al-Da'im (d. 1908 CE). Since it was commonly accepted by the Sufis that one could not make spiritual progress without the aid of a competent guide, Muhammad Ahmad joined the *sammaniyah tariqa*. As the famous Persian Sufi Bayazid Bistami once remarked, 'One who has no guide has taken *shaytan* (Satan) as his guide.' Muhammad Ahmad agreed with this view and became a loyal follower of Shaykh al-Da'im who guided him along the spiritual path for around five years until he attained the rank of a Shaykh himself. He was only twenty-two at the time.

Unlike the majority of the Sufis of his time, Muhammad Ahmad's understanding of spirituality combined both spirituality and social and political activism. That is to say, his early training in Islamic theology, jurisprudence and spirituality encouraged him to lead a basic and ascetic lifestyle. But, at the same time, following in the footsteps of the Prophet, he married and set up his own family. He was only twenty-four when he built a new mosque and Sufi *zawiyah* (lodge) to spread Islamic moral, ethical and spiritual teachings. Likewise, he encouraged his people to seek Islamic knowledge and wisdom within Sudan, rather than go abroad to study at prominent Islamic institutions like al-Azhar University. As a bright student, he could have gone to al-Azhar if he wanted, but Muhammad Ahmad decided to stay in Sudan and help revive Islamic principles and practices in that country. When his family left Karari in 1870 CE and moved to Aba Island in search of timber so they could continue their boat-making business, Muhammad Ahmad joined them.

Here he married for the second time and his fame began to spread throughout the island on account of his vast knowledge and understanding of Islam. He then established a Sufi lodge and gathered around him a small band of followers. By coincidence, Shaykh al-Da'im, his former teacher and spiritual guide, also moved to an adjacent town. He became jealous of his former pupil's popularity with the locals. Soon the two men clashed. Muhammad Ahmad was formally expelled from the *sammaniyah* Order by Shaykh al-Da'im himself. Infuriated by the latter's snub, Muhammad Ahmad went and pledged allegiance to Shaykh Quraishi who was a master of another branch of *sammaniyah* Sufi Order and strengthened his ties with the latter by marrying his daughter. Following Shaykh Quraishi's death in 1878 CE, Muhammad Ahmad succeeded him as the leader of this Sufi branch and his reputation began to spread across the wider region.

As a religious leader and spiritual guide, his main priority was to promote Islamic education and improve the social and economic condition of his people. Since Sudan was an Ottoman-Egyptian colony at the time, the country's colonial rulers failed to exercise proper political leadership. They also did not seem to have any plans to improve the Sudanese people's social and economic conditions. The ruling elite's failure to tackle the people's socio-economic problems and difficulties eventually led to widespread resentment across the country. Prompted by the colonialists' disinterest in the suffering of the people, he began to preach a new form of religious activism. He emphasised the importance of personal purification and rectitude, along with the need for social morality, collective responsibility and political activism across Sudan. While Muhammad Ahmad was busy formulating his new religious and political ideology – underpinned by Islamic principles and practices – a man named Abdullahi ibn Muhammad (b. 1846-d. 1899 CE), who originated from the province of Kordofan, came to visit him in 1880 CE.

The two men instantly became close friends and resolved to work together for the political, economic and spiritual betterment of their people. Even before Abdullahi's arrival, Muhammad Ahmad told some of his close disciples that he was the long-awaited Mahdi (the 'centenarian renewer of faith'). The East Africans expected the Mahdi to arrive during the thirteenth century of Islam and help them liberate their land from foreign occupation. After his arrival, Abdullahi convinced Muhammad Ahmad that he was indeed that 'renewer of faith' long expected by his countrymen. Muhammad was urged on by Abdullahi. He then announced that he had been blessed with a series of visions wherein he was informed that he was the expected Mahdi. He reinforced his claim to Mahdihood by reinterpreting the Prophetic *Hadith* concerning the emergence of Imam Mahdi towards the end of time.

As the self-proclaimed saviour of his people, he now began to tour Sudan to propagate Islam and establish his authority as the spiritual and political leader of his people. His call for political unity and a return to the original, pure teachings of Islam went down well with the public. Having suffered decades of political oppression and economic hardship under foreign rule, the Sudanese people gave him a warm reception. As his followers began to increase rapidly, Muhammad Ahmad criticised the oppressive policies of the colonial rulers. It was not long before his religious and political opposition against the colonialists won him widespread support in Sudan. Indeed, soon a mass anti-colonial movement began to take shape. Although he was not a politician, Muhammad Ahmad's authority as a leader of his people surpassed such categorisation.

As it was, the religious and political strategy he pursued in Sudan was very similar to that championed by the Prophet Muhammad back in seventh-century Arabia. Like the Prophet, he asked his followers to pledge *bay'ah* (loyalty) to him. He also performed a *hijrah* (migration) from Aba Island to Jabal Qadir in the same way the Prophet migrated from Makkah to Madinah. Finally, he named his supporters *al-ansar* (the helpers) just as the Prophet had. Being thoroughly familiar with the *sira* (life and teachings of the prophet), Muhammad Ahmad followed a reformist method which he believed was Divinely inspired, like the mission of the Prophet Muhammad.

However, when he and his disciples began to intensify their religious and political activities, the Khartoum-based Ottoman-Egyptian rulers became very alarmed. They tried to calm down Muhammad Ahmad's followers (known as the *mahdiyah*) by agreeing to some of their demands, but he rejected them in no uncertain terms. After some deliberation, the authorities in Khartoum decided to launch a military action against the *mahdiyah*. Thus, in 1882 CE, two successive military expeditions were sent by the Egyptian forces against the *mahdiyah* in which the latter inflicted a crushing defeat on the Egyptian army.

The unexpected success of the *mahdiyah* won Muhammad Ahmad widespread recognition throughout Sudan, and more and more people responded to his call for national religious and political unity and solidarity. Encouraged by their success, the *mahdiyah* then advanced towards central Kordafan where they received a warm reception from the locals and laid siege to the town of al-Ubayyid (El-Obeid). After capturing the town in 1883 CE, Muhammad Ahmad became the undisputed ruler of Kordofan and its neighbouring territories.

As a charismatic leader and an electrifying orator, he inspired his followers to pursue *jihad* (military struggle) against their enemies. He promised to lead them all the way to Makkah and Madinah, two of Islam's most sacred cities, via Cairo. Muhammad Ahmad and his *mahdiyah* became so powerful that they eventually captured Khartoum in 1885 CE after inflicting a crushing defeat on the forces of Charles George Gordon, a British military general, who died fighting on the battlefield. Although General Gordon's defeat at the hands of the Sudanese revolutionary army created a huge political storm in Britain at the time, Muhammad Ahmad and his forces went on to reunite the whole country under his leadership. However, six months after establishing himself in Omdurman, which became the new capital of Sudan, he suddenly died of fever at the age of forty.

Within a short time, he managed to unite his people under the banner of Islam and forced out the combined might of the Ottoman, Egyptian and British armies from his country. After abolishing the tribal customs and traditions which prevailed in Sudan at the time, he propagated the *Sharia* (Islamic law) across the country. By doing this, he initiated a process of Islamisation and Arabisation which subsequently spread across all Sudan and East Africa. Though the *mahdiyah* State established by Muhammad Ahmad was destroyed by an Anglo-Egyptian army barely fourteen years after its beginning, his influence and legacy continue to play a powerful role in Sudanese politics to this day. Although his claim to have been the Mahdi was rightly rejected by the orthodox Muslims, his contribution to the Islamic revival and recovery in the Sudan and East Africa was nothing short of remarkable. For this reason, he deserves to be recognised as one of the most influential *mujahid* (Islamic warrior) of modern times.

He is regarded as the 'father of modern Sudan'. Muhammad Ahmad's legacy later inspired his son, Sir Sayyid Abd al-Rahman al-Mahdi (b. 1885-d. 1959 CE), to establish the *ummah* party (a national Sudanese political and religious party) in 1945 CE. The party was led by his grandson, Sayyid Sadiq al-Mahdi (b. 1935-d. 2020 CE). The party continues to exert considerable political influence in Sudan to this day. Internationally, however, Muhammad Ahmad's heroic struggle against the colonial powers turned him into a powerful symbol of pride and prestige among Black nationalists across Africa, Europe and the United States.

92

*Muhammad Abduh
(b.1849 - d.1905 CE) /
(b.1266 - d.1323 AH)*

The nineteenth century was one of the most politically traumatic and intellectually deteriorating periods in the history of Islam. Historically speaking, as and when the Muslim world surrendered to the attractions and luxuries of materialism or went through a period of intellectual inaction, influential religious reformers or political leaders emerged to warn the public and call them back to the original, pure message of Islam. Thus, during the Umayyad period, Hasan al-Basri (see chapter 15) and Umar ibn Abd al-Aziz (see chapter 19) emerged to warn the public of the dangers of uncontrolled power, greed and pleasure-seeking. Ahmad ibn Hanbal (see chapter 31) and his successors did the same during the Abbasid period. Later, as intellectual confusion and moral corruption began to raise their ugly heads in the eleventh century, towering figures like Ibn Hazm (see chapter 53) and Imam al-Ghazali (see chapter 56) appeared to defend traditional Islam.

In the middle of the chaos created by the Mongols in the thirteenth century, Imam al-Nawawi (see chapter 71) and Ibn Taymiyyah (see chapter 72) attempted to revive the *minhaj al-Sunnah* (Prophetic practices and methodology). Likewise, in the sixteenth century, Shaykh Ahmad Sirhindi (see chapter 81), the influential Indian Muslim reformer, and Muhammad ibn Pir Ali (b. 1522-d. 1573 CE), better known as Imam Birgivi, the renowned Turkish Islamic scholar and Sufi sage, emerged to champion Islamic moral, ethical and spiritual teachings for the benefit of their people.

The rise of Muhammad ibn Abd al-Wahhab (see chapter 85) in Arabia and the pan-Islamic reformer and activist Jamal al-Din 'al-Afghani' (see chapter 90), in the eighteenth and nineteenth centuries respectively, proved that Islam was capable of renewing itself in times of crises. It also paved the way for Muhammad Abduh, an outstanding disciple of 'al-Afghani' and the 'father of Islamic modernism' to emerge and become one of the most influential Islamic thinkers and reformers of the nineteenth century.

Muhammad Abduh was born in a village in northern Egypt close to the Nile. Abduh's father was a relatively well-off trader of some position in his locality. Young Abduh was brought up in the traditional atmosphere of the Nile Delta. He showed signs of unusual intellectual ability from an early age. His family was keen to educate and support him so they admitted him to his local village *maktab* (religious school) where he committed the entire Qur'an to memory, which won him much praise from his teachers. Impressed by his rapid progress, Abduh's family then enrolled him at the noted Ahmadi mosque and seminary in Tanta at the age of thirteen. Here he received further education in Arabic language, grammar, literature and traditional Islamic sciences. Thanks to his ability to retain and absorb vast quantities of information, he completed his further and intermediate education.

During his time at this institute, Abduh developed a keen interest in the speculative sciences, including philosophy and spirituality. He then enrolled at *Jamia al-Azhar* (al-Azhar University) in Cairo to pursue higher education in Arabic literature, logic, philosophy and mysticism. Al-Azhar was originally founded by the Fatimids (fl. 909-1171 CE) in the tenth century. It is one of the world's oldest institutions of higher education and one of the Muslim world's most famous seats of Islamic learning and scholarship. Abduh excelled in his studies, passing his final examinations with flying colours at the age of twenty-six. On account of his great talent and intellectual ability, the university authorities asked him to stay on and teach the undergraduate students. For the next two years, he lectured at al-Azhar and became a popular figure due to his great learning and refreshing approach to Islam.

As a lecturer at al-Azhar, he first met Jamal al-Din 'al-Afghani', the famous Muslim thinker and pan-Islamic politician of the nineteenth century. Abduh found 'al-Afghani' to be an inspirational intellectual, captivating lecturer and highly motivated political activist who developed a new and original pan-Islamic political ideology to unify the Muslim world under the banner of Islam. Since a large part of the Muslim world was suffering under European colonial rule at the time, Abduh was convinced that 'al-Afghani's' rallying call for Islamic unity and solidarity was the only way the Muslims could liberate their lands from foreign occupation.

Though 'al-Afghani's' message of Islamic unity and solidarity never went down well with the colonial rulers (whether in India, Egypt or for that matter Ottoman Turkey), here at al-Azhar his call for Islamic political unity won him a large following. The British were alarmed by 'al-Afghani's' ideological interpretation of Islam. They exercised real political power in Egypt at the time, so they expelled him from the country in 1879 CE. Before being thrown out, 'al-Afghani' had managed to plant the seeds of pan-Islamic thinking in the intellectual circles of Cairo. Abduh would continue to oversee the development of the pan-Islamic movement in that country.

Following 'al-Afghani's' expulsion from Egypt, Abduh returned to his native village, probably to allow the dust of the political storm which raged in Cairo to settle. After returning to the capital he took up the post of editor of *al-Waqa'i al-Misriyah* (The Egyptian Gazette) which was a government publication. In this Gazette, he published scores of articles, calling for Islamic unity and the need for social, political and religious reform in Egypt. The voices of nationalism became louder by the day after the formal British military occupation of Egypt in 1882 CE. It was during this period that Abduh fell out with the British authorities for supporting the nationalists. He was forced to live in exile for about six years. But from his safe haven in Lebanon, he continued his opposition to the British.

He also found time to establish a modern Islamic school to train students in both traditional Islamic sciences and modern philosophical thought. Despite being brought up in a traditional environment – and having also received a thorough education in traditional Islamic sciences –Abduh had a modern mindset. He was also very eager to explore the political and intellectual problems faced by the Islamic world at the time. He found the Egyptian educational system far too didactic, cumbersome and uninspiring. Moreover, he felt the absence of political unity, social progress and intellectual creativity in Egypt and the rest of the Muslim world had undermined the people's confidence, self-belief and collective will to face the social, political, economic and intellectual challenges posed by Western modernity and secularism.

He was convinced that the traditional methods of teaching the Islamic sciences did not promote intellectual creativity and fresh thinking, which was the cornerstone of modern Western educational philosophy. Thus he began to rethink his entire approach to Islam. The answers to the challenges of Western modernity were unlikely to come from the fortress of Islamic traditionalism. This was because, in his opinion, the champions of traditionalism were determined to cling to their outmoded religious methods. Likewise, an entirely modernistic approach to Islam was not the answer either, because he felt this could lead to a rapid dilution of the essentials of Islam.

Abduh concluded that combining the traditional methods of teaching Islamic sciences with a modern approach was the only sustainable alternative. This would enable Islamic institutions to produce a new generation of Islamic scholars, intellectuals and reformers who could tackle the challenges which confronted the Muslim world at the time. A few years later, Abduh left Beirut for Paris where he joined forces with 'al-Afghani', his former mentor and guide, to bring about political change and reform in the Muslim world.

Both were shocked by the dilemma and difficulty of the Muslim *ummah* (global community). So the master and student worked tirelessly to reform Islamic thought and reawaken the Muslim world from its deep slumber. In Paris, they established an institute for social and political reform in the Muslim world and published their famous journal *al-Urwa al-Wuthqa* (The Unbreakable Bond). This phrase appears twice in the Qur'an and refers to those people who place their absolute trust in Divine power and judgement. Through this journal, Abduh and his mentor launched a blistering intellectual assault on the European colonial powers, especially the British who at the time exercised power in India and Egypt.

These countries soon became the main focus of their political confrontation. Their call for the masses to rise against the colonial powers and liberate their lands from Western domination, instantly turned Abduh and 'al-Afghani' into heroic figures in many parts of the Muslim world. Although 'al-Afghani' was a powerful thinker who possessed an encyclopaedic mind, unfortunately, he exhausted much of his physical and intellectual energy in uncoordinated social and political activism.

By contrast, Abduh sought to explore and rethink the entire Islamic intellectual framework to devise a new educational method which would be relevant to his time. In so doing he hoped to combat the forces of Westernisation and secularism which threatened to overwhelm the Muslim world. Abduh and 'al-Afghani's' political ideas and religious thoughts struck a chord with the public in many parts of the Muslim world. In response, the British authorities in Egypt imposed a ban on their journal. But it was regularly smuggled into the country where it acquired a large following. After publishing only eighteen issues, the journal expired due to lack of funding, censorship and political restrictions. Yet, within a relatively short period, it had created a huge political stir in the Muslim world.

After the end of *al-Urwa al-Wuthqa* in 1884 CE, Abduh left Paris and returned to Beirut where he gathered around him a number of talented young intellectuals and activists, including Muhammad Rashid Rida (b. 1865-d. 1935 CE). Rida became one of his most able and trusted disciples. Abduh then lost contact with 'al-Afghani' and the political situation in his native Egypt began to improve. So the British authorities allowed him to return to Cairo in 1888 CE. Now considered to be an outstanding Islamic thinker and jurist, he was appointed a *qadi* (judge). Over the next decade, Abduh changed and re-formulated his views on many aspects of Islam and worked tirelessly to develop a balanced approach to Islamic thought and jurisprudence in light of his observed condition.

He wrote scores of articles, treatises and a partial commentary on the Qur'an, entitled *Tafsir al-Manar* (Interpretation of the Beacon), which was later completed and published in 1927 CE by Rashid Rida. Abduh always expressed his views on Islam and Islamic jurisprudence in a clear and forthright manner. His most famous book was *Risalat al-Tawhid* (A Treatise on Divine Unity) in which he developed a fresh and challenging explanation of

Islamic philosophy and theology in the light of Western modernity. According to Abduh, although *aql* (reason) and *wahy* (revelation) are two distinct sources of knowledge, they are not contradictory. Rather they are two complementary sources of knowledge. As such, both reason and revelation are necessary for developing a comprehensive and authentic interpretation of Islamic philosophical, theological, ethical and legal thought. Much confusion and chaos, he argued, had become set in the Muslim mind and morals due to the Islamic scholar's failure to relate the fundamental principles of Islam to their current realities. In other words, Abduh believed that the universal principles of Islam are timeless and unchangeable, but our current condition constantly changes and evolves. Thus, the principles of Islam must always underpin our personal as well as collective actions.

His reformist (or modernist) approach to Islamic thought and jurisprudence led him to refute the practice of *taqlid* (uncritical imitation of tradition). Instead, as a *mufti* (Islamic jurist-consult), he argued in favour of *ijtihad* (exercising individual scholarly judgement). He was influenced by the 'critical jurisprudence' of al-Shatibi (b. 1320-d. 1388 CE), the famous Andalusian Islamic jurist. So Abduh believed it was the Muslim failure to exercise *ijtihad* continuously which helped to create the unfavourable circumstances in which the Muslim world found itself at the time. Blind or uncritical imitation of tradition not only undermined the Muslim's self-belief and confidence but also reduced all forms of creativity and fresh thinking among Muslim scholars and intellectuals.

To refresh the Muslim mind and regenerate Islamic societies, he, like al-Shatibi, called for a return to the original sources of Islam, namely the Qur'an and the authentic *Sunnah* (Prophetic practice). A fresh approach to, and understanding of, the two fundamental scriptural sources of Islam would, he felt, enable the Muslims to break out of the cycle of intellectual poverty, social degeneration and political domination, and usher in a new era of peace, and progress and development across the Muslim world.

After working as a judge for about a decade, in 1899 CE Abduh was appointed Grand Mufti of Egypt. This was the highest judicial post in the country. He also became a member of the Egyptian Legislative Council. During his period as Grand Mufti, he carried out much-needed reform of the judicial system and sponsored the publication of the renowned journal *al-manar* (The Beacon). It was founded by his disciple Muhammad Rashid Rida back in 1898 CE. Six years after becoming the Grand Mufti, Abduh died at the age of fifty-four and was buried in Cairo.

However, his religious ideas and thoughts continued to be championed for another three decades by Rashid Rida, who also authored a comprehensive biography of Abduh under the title of *Tarikh al-Ustadh al-Imam Muhammad Abduh*. His essays and articles, consisting of five volumes, were published separately. His efforts to reconcile the timeless values and principles of Islam with the new challenges and realities of his time earned Abduh much praise from his admirers as well as criticism from many religious   conservatives.

However, as the 'father of Islamic modernism', his reformist ideas and thoughts have influenced generations of Islamic scholars, thinkers and reformers across the Muslim world, especially in Egypt, India and Indonesia, including Mawlana Abul Kalam Azad (b. 1888-d. 1958 CE), Mawlana Muhammad Akram Khan (b. 1868-d. 1969 CE), Leopold Weiss (b. 1900-d. 1992 CE) (Muhammad Asad), and Abd al-Malik Karim Amrullah (1908-d. 1981 CE), otherwise known as 'Hamka' in the Far East.

93

Nawab Sultan Jahan Begum (b.1858 - d.1930 CE) / (b.1275 - d.1349 AH)

The most splendid century in the history of the state of Bhopal is proclaimed by visionary women. This princely state was ruled by four women from 1819 to 1926 CE. These were Kudsia Begum, Sikander Begum, Shah Jahan Begum and Sultan Jahan Begum. Bhopal was first established in central India in 1724 CE and was an independent state before it became a British protectorate in 1818 CE. The state then unified with independent India in 1949 CE and is now part of Madhya Pradesh.

The Sultan was the only surviving child of her mother, Shah Jahan Begum Sahiba, by her first husband, General Nawab Baqi Muhammad Khan Bahadur. Sultan Jahan Begum was born on 19th July 1858 CE. She was the last of four women *nawabs* (governors) who ruled Bhopal during the British Raj. All of these Begums were highly capable administrators and women of courage and determination. They eventually became sources of inspiration for their family, communities and women in general.

Others had become governors at a younger age, but Sultan Jahan Begum, at the age of fourty-three, was the oldest of them to ascend the throne. For a few years, there was a disagreement between her mother and herself. This difference divided loyalties in the court, each with its own supporters. But as a ruler, she ensured that upright rules and a fair administrative system were implemented. She set an example of good governance by instructing her judicial officials to administer justice to everyone by making the commands of Allah their guidance.

The Sultan was a religious and pious Muslimah. In 1903-1904 CE, she went for *hajj*. At that time, Hijaz was under Ottoman rule. She wrote a book about her journey, The Story of a Pilgrimage to Hijaz. In it, she narrated the events which first took her and her entourage by land to Mumbai (previously Bombay). From there, their group boarded a steamer to Aden, Jeddah and the port of Yanbu on the Red Sea. From there, the party travelled on camels under Turkish military protection to Madinah and Makkah. On her return to Bhopal, there was a huge celebration for her accomplishment of an important pillar of Islam. The minarets of many mosques were decorated and lit in her respect. The relics that she had collected from Makkah and Madinah were displayed for the public to see.

Sultan Jahan Begum was a prolific writer and through her writing, she influenced the public and the learned. The scrutiny of her work was very sharp. She reviewed her own scripts and marked her mistakes. She authored the biography of her relatives and her autobiography in three volumes. The English title is called 'An Account of My Life'. She wrote about fifty books on different subjects including cooking, housekeeping, health, women's rights and responsibilities, nurturing children and others. She loved poetry and the arts. She gave speeches about female education at female conventions, which were compiled into a book in 1919 CE. Her other speeches and writings were published in women's Urdu journals.

The Begums were very proud and appreciative of their mothers and grandmothers. They paid their tribute and respect to the powerful women who influenced their personalities. It is noted that their devotion to Islam and simplicity set them apart from the other royal lives of luxury, extravagance and idleness. These women often referred to the Qur'an and reputable Islamic scholars to uphold the belief that Islam promotes gender equality.

One of the best, and most famous and authentic biographies of the Prophet Muhammad in Urdu is *Sirat-Un-Nabi* (Life of the Prophet) by Allamah Shibli Nomani. It has been translated into English as well. Sultan Jahan Begum was very interested in history and had great love for Prophet Muhammad. She financed the publication of this voluminous book. She continued to support the project after the death of Allamah Shibli Nomani when his disciple Maulana Syed Sulaiman Nadwi wrote the rest and completed it. She made such a huge contribution that some believe that if Allah wills, this monumental effort will please the Prophet on the Day of Judgment so that he will intercede with Allah to forgive her.

At all times and with everyone, she conducted herself courteously and spoke gently and politely so much so that sometimes people forgot that they were conversing and listening to a *nawab*. Her personality was a balance between that of command and affection. Her court showed simplicity, and the manners of the court were in accordance with the teachings of Islam. On the throne, she would take her seat behind a curtain. Grand salutations and excessive veneration were shunned in her court. Upon arriving at the court, she would always greet with 'Aslsalamu Alaykum' in an audible voice. When she spoke and deliberated her matters, everyone would be impressed by her educated and cultured talk.

She conducted the administration of the state with her son, Nawab Muhammad Nasrullah Khan. The Sultan observed the veil proudly and confidently even when she was around dignitaries of the government, fellow rulers, foreign leaders, the British governor and viceroy. She received all of them from behind a curtain. In politics, she was an intelligent and courageous negotiator with the British government and always protected the interests of her family and her state. Sultan Jahan Begum met the Royal Highnesses the Prince and Princess of Wales at Indore in 1905 CE where she was awarded the Order of Chivalry, Knight Grand Commander.

King Edward VII of England died in 1910 CE, and George V was to be crowned as the new King. The Coronation was going to be held in London and Sultan Jahan Begum was invited to it. She attended the Coronation of George V and Queen Mary at Westminster Abbey in 1911 CE. She attended it dressed in a *burqa*. She was intensely pro-British and proudly displayed her medals and awards for her services to the British Empire on the outside of her clothing.

Sultan Jahan Begum was very aware of her times and the needs of her role. She was excellent at balancing the requirements of Islam and the cultural elements of Western civiliszations, and from this point of view, she was regarded as a model by reformists.

Her religious and cultural education was perfect whereas her Western knowledge was as it was necessary.

There are some magnificent buildings that she beautified Bhopal with. Some of these include Qaser-e-Sultani Palace, which now houses the Saifia College and Noor-us-Sabah Palace, which is a heritage hotel. Minto Hall housed the Madhya Pradesh Vidhan Sabha until 1996 CE. Then there is the Edward Museum and Hamidia Library. The Jehan Numa Palace built by Nawab Sultan Jahan Begum was given to her son, General Obaidullah Khan. In September 1983 CE, the Palace was opened as a heritage palace hotel to visitors. In 2000 CE, the Palace was classified as a Heritage Grand Hotel, the first in Central India. It is said that the menu at the Jahan Numa Palace has recipes that have been passed down through generations. Many were inspired by the dishes served at the banquets during the reign of Shah Jahan Begum. The Jehan Numa Palace has also opened a museum highlighting the history of Bhopal through pictures and some memories. Sikander Begum had permitted to construction of a Catholic Church, which is now a Cathedral. Sultan Jahan also founded the Archaeological Museum built in 1919 CE and together with her mother, Sultan Jahan Begum, financed the preservation of the ancient Buddhist Stupa at Sanchi.

Jahan Begum promoted professionalisation concerning female health practitioners and medical institutions. She took responsibility for her state's women's clinics and dispensaries while also developing a training curriculum for Unani doctors, nurses and midwives. To reform society, increase prosperity and progress the civic bodies, she totally changed the tax system, army, police, judiciary and prisons. She expanded agriculture and improved public sanitation, hygiene and health using widespread inoculation and vaccination programmes. These became part of the Women's Health Reforms program. Sultan Jahan expanded trade and business by building towns and creating jobs. All this positioned Bhopal as an important state on India's map.

Although she constructed many impressive buildings, her real concern and passion was to build the life and character of her people. To achieve this objective she focussed on education, especially women's education. Begum Sultan Jahan paid particular attention to women's education and supported Mohammad Girls School of Aligarh started by Shaykh Abdullah. The school was searching for an acceptable curriculum, but the lack of funds was a challenge. Sultan Jahan donated generously to develop a curriculum for women's education and presented its outline ats a Presidential address at the annual Muslim Educational Conference in 1911 CE. During her visit to Aligarh in 1915 CE, she inaugurated the girls' school building and laid the foundation stone for the girl's' hostel.

In 1900 CE, she built the Hamidia Library founded by her third son Hamidullah Khan. The library hugely influenced and inspired students and academics. Like the three previous Begums, Sultan Jahan founded many educational establishments and sponsored many public schools. In these schools, regular moral and civil education courses were a very important part of state education. She also initiated an art school in the year 1905 CE for widows and destitute women.

However, until today, her greatest legacy is the Aligarh Muslim University which came into being in 1920 CE. She became the founding Chancellor of Aligarh Muslim University and the first Indian woman to become a Chancellor of an Indian University. Sultan Jahan supported the Scientific Society by donating a large sum of money to M. A. O. College Jama Masjid construction. Begum Sultan Jahan was very much supportive of the vision and mission of Sir Syed Ahmad Khan.

From 1901 to 1926 CE, the Begum ruled the Indian Princely State of Bhopal. Her reign lasted more than twenty-five years. She abdicated the throne to her son Muhammed Habibullah Khan. At the crowning ceremony of the new ruler, she addressed the audience that it had been twenty-five years since Allah had given her the rule of the state. She informed them that all her decisions to introduce changes were in the best interest of the people. She said that she had been sincere and that she did all she could for the welfare of the public. She did not leave any stone unturned to apply the rules of Allah Who blessed her with His favours, which resulted in the prosperity of Bhopal everywhere.

Before concluding her speech, she advised the new ruler. She then recited from the Qur'an in which it has been commanded that justice be administered for everyone, to help the poor, orphans, needy and strangers abstain from wrongdoings and headstrongness, establish regular prayers and fulfil all the promises. Then the new ruler was seated on the throne. She raised her hands and made the following *du'a* (prayer) from the Qur'an:

> My Lord, enable me to be grateful for Your favour which You have bestowed upon me and upon my parents and to righteous work righteousness of which You will approve and make righteous for me my offspring. Indeed, I have repented to You, and indeed, I am of the Muslims. (AhqafAhzab, 4633:15).

She was crying profusely while she was praying, and the audience wept with her. Four years later, on 13th May 1930 CE, she died. The Muslims all over the world felt the shock of her death.

Bhopal was a unique princely state because it had been ruled by a succession of widows. Sultan Jahan Begum was a highly skilled politician and social reformer. She took great strides in improving the condition of the people of Bhopal, especially women. Her life and contributions are strongly felt and appreciated by the people of Bhopal and those in other lands.

Sultan Jahan Begum was a fantastic visionary and a kind-hearted person. However, her main legacy was public health, inoculation, vaccination, improving sanitation, hygiene and the water supply. However, her greatest contribution was in education at a time when the concept of women's empowerment was minimal. She was not only a ruler and leader of Indian women but the chancellor of the only Muslim university at the time. But above her administrative, national, scholarly and educational achievements, her real honour lies in her devotion to Islam, love for her religion and spiritual closeness to Allah.

94

Abd al-Aziz ibn Saud (b.1875 - d.1953 CE) / (b.1292 - d.1373 AH)

Muhammad ibn Saud (d. 1765 CE), the charismatic founder of the Saudi dynasty (also known as the House of Saud), was born around 1685 CE. After succeeding his father as the ruler of the oasis region of Diriyyah at the age of forty, he allied with Muhammad ibn Abd al-Wahhab (see chapter 85), the renowned Islamic scholar and reformer of Arabia, in 1744 CE. They laid the foundations of the modern Saudi State. A supporter of traditional Islam, Muhammad ibn Saud's agreement with Ibn Abd al-Wahhab stated that Islam was to be the basis of the new sState. This gave him the religious justification for his rule. They were of the same age and had a similar understanding and approach to Islam. The two Muhammads thus joined together to create a powerful political and religious partnership in Arabia.

To further strengthen their relationship, Muhammad ibn Saud married Ibn Abd al-Wahhab's daughter, which brought the two families even closer together. They shared the political and religious leadership of the country. The first Saudi State was established around 1744 CE and it lasted until it was destroyed in 1818 CE by the forces of Muhammad Ali Pasha (b. 1769-d. 1849 CE), the powerful Ottoman viceroy of Egypt. Then in 1824 CE, another political and religious order emerged in Arabia which was modelled on the first Saudi State. However nonstop internal conflict and political rivalry led to its breakup in 1891 CE. However, the credit for laying the foundations of the Kingdom of Saudi Arabia, the modern Saudi State, must go to Abd al-Aziz ibn Saud, who was undoubtedly one of the most charismatic and influential Arab leaders of modern times.

Abd al-Aziz ibn Abd al-Rahman ibn Faisal al-Saud, known as Ibn Saud for short, was born in Riyadh, the capital of modern Saudi Arabia, but he spent his early years in Kuwait. After Abd al-Rahman ibn Faisal (b. 1845-d. 1928 CE), the father of Ibn Saud, competed with his three brothers over the right to political succession, his family became divided. This strengthened the hands of their opponents. Abd al-Rahman ibn Faisal was frustrated by his battles with his brothers. He was eventually forced to leave Arabia after Riyadh was captured by Muhammad ibn Abdullah al-Rashid, the ruler of Najd and a political rival of the al-Saud family. During his exile in Kuwait, however, Ibn Saud maintained close contact with his supporters back home, hoping one day to return to his native Riyadh in triumph.

Young Ibn Saud grew up in Kuwait, living among the bedouins and learning the art of surviving in the dry and harsh environment of the desert. He studied the Qur'an and religious sciences during his early years and became familiar with the basic principles and practices of Islam. He then received training in desert warfare and soon became an expert in launching military raids. Tall, handsome and charismatic, Ibn Saud also became a clever political strategist and a talented military general. Living in the desert with the bedouins made him very tough, resilient and skilful. Moreover, his years of training in military strategy and desert warfare equipped him with much-needed skills to organise and launch military expeditions to reclaim his ancestral homeland from his rivals. From exile in Kuwait, he and his family thus waited patiently for the right moment to strike against their rivals in Arabia.

The British had established their political and economic influence across much of Arabia long before the twentieth century. Their political and economic control of the region came under direct threat from other leading European powers (including France and Germany) at the beginning of the twentieth century. Even after

Kuwait became a British protectorate in 1899 CE, they struggled to protect their political and economic interests in the region from German and French invasions. The British were keen to maintain their regional interests, so they fought vigorously against their European rivals to keep them out of the Middle East. While the Europeans were busy competing with one another to increase their influence across the Arabian Peninsula, Ibn Saud's ancestral home remained firmly in the grip of the Rashidi rulers who at the time were actively supported by the Ottomans.

Following the death of the charismatic Rashidi ruler Muhammad ibn Abdullah al-Rashid in 1897 CE, Riyadh was rocked by both political disturbance and social disturbances. The situation deteriorated further as his successor, Abd al-Aziz ibn Mithab, ruthlessly suppressed the uprising. As expected, his heavy-handed policy created much anger and hatred. This led the locals to engage in uprising activities against the ruling elites, which, in turn, led to more political chaos and anarchy in Arabia. Despite the volatile situation at home, the new Rashidi ruler – supported by the Ottomans – launched an unprovoked attack on Kuwait, which was still then a British protectorate. But thanks to the British, the Rashidi ruler's attempt to capture Kuwait failed miserably.

Indeed, Ibn Mithab's attack on Kuwait backfired spectacularly. Shaykh al-Mubarak al-Saba, the ruler of Kuwait, and Abd al-Rahman ibn Faisal, the father of Ibn Saud, now united to drive out the Rashidis from Arabia. Leading a ten thousand-strong force, the two men attacked the Rashidi forces with great success. During this period the twenty-two-year-old Ibn Saud spearheaded the attack on Riyadh, his home city.

He left Kuwait with his brother, Muhammad, along with a band of around forty determined fighters and quickly reached the borders of Riyadh where they camped under the cover of darkness. Ten trustworthy supporters joined him and together he then entered Riyadh during the night and launched a surprise attack on the forces of the local governor. In the battle, the city's governor was slain by Abdullah ibn Jelawi, Ibn Saud's cousin. They inflicted a crushing defeat on their enemy. The fall of Riyadh marked the beginning of the end for the Rashidi family. The House of Saud swiftly returned its authority across the country under the able stewardship of Ibn Saud and his father.

The capture of Riyadh by young Ibn Saud strengthened his reputation as an able political strategist and military commander. It also won him much-deserved praise from both his family members and the people. Thereafter, he urged the local religious leaders and the people of Riyadh to pledge allegiance to his father, Abd al-Rahman ibn Faisal, as their new sovereign. The people responded to his call and pledged their allegiance to him. Later, Ibn Saud's popularity and standing with the public prompted his father to abdicate in favour of his son, who accordingly became the King.

With Riyadh now firmly in his grip, Ibn Saud was eager to extend his rule across the rest of Arabia. But he knew it was not an easy task because the Rashidis were in full control in Najd. Thus, he decided to strengthen his political position and authority by entering into a series of strategic alliances through marriage. In fiercely tribal and polygamous societies, political rulers and religious scholars often extended their social ties and strengthened their political power and position in society through multiple marriages. Early twentieth-century Arabia was no different in this respect, and Ibn Saud understood this better than anyone else. Thus, over the next five decades, he married more than a dozen times, fathering around forty sons and fifty daughters. Even in a society where multiple marriages were very common; his excess surprised his friends and family alike.

But, as a clever politician, he knew that forming alliances through multiple marriages not only helped to extend his family ties but also strengthened his political power base. At the same time, he was aware that having a large family alone did not guarantee success on the battlefield. To win in the theatre of war, he had to create a strong, unified and disciplined army. Accordingly, in 1912 CE, he established a special fighting force which came to be known as the *ikhwan* (the Brotherhood). The members of this force were loyal supporters of the House of Saud and strict adherents of Islam as interpreted by Muhammad ibn Abd al-Wahhab.

With the support of the *ikhwan* troops, Ibn Saud first conquered the wealthy region of Hasa (situated on the coast of the Persian Gulf) and then went on to smash the Rashidis of Najd in 1921 CE. Five years later, he expelled the Hashimites from the Hijaz. Thus he extended his rule and authority over the holy cities of Makkah and Madinah which brought him much-needed revenue for his growing administration from the visiting pilgrims. After concluding his military campaigns, Ibn Saud struggled to control his over-enthusiastic *ikhwan* troops who wanted to carry out continuous *jihad* (military struggle) against their enemies. Ibn Saud was not keen on pursuing endless military conquests, so he swiftly disbanded the *ikhwan* and focused his full attention on improving the economic fortunes of his new kingdom. If founding the new Saudi State was a hard struggle, then ruling the affairs of the State proved to be even more challenging for Ibn Saud because some of the territories he conquered had no proper political or administrative structures in place at all.

In response, he established a Council of Ministers to oversee the affairs of the state and appointed close members of his family to key positions within the government. Thus, his two eldest sons, Saud ibn Abd al-Aziz (b. 1902-d. 1969 CE) and Faisal ibn Abd al-Aziz (b. 1906-d. 1975 CE), were offered high-ranking government posts in the province of Najd and Hijaz. Despite being heavily in debt – and unable to obtain external financial assistance – he nevertheless established a Ministry of Finance to tackle the kingdom's financial problems. During this period, he also applied the *Sharia* (Islamic law) across the State and shortly afterwards this became the supreme law of the land.

Then, in 1930 CE, Ibn Saud established a Ministry of Foreign Affairs and appointed his second son, Faisal, as Foreign Minister. Faisal played a key role in establishing diplomatic relations with some of the world's leading powers, including the United States of America. Two years later, the formation of the Kingdom of Saudi Arabia was officially announced. This was followed, in the mid-1930s, by the discovery of the world's largest oil reserves beneath the barren deserts of Arabia. This completely transformed the political and economic fortunes of Saudi Arabia and instantly catapulted the Saudi Kingdom onto the global stage. Then, by the 1940s, Saudi Arabia's diplomatic relations with the powerful industrial Western nations (especially the United States) were formalised. Ibn Saud was keen to export the vast quantities of oil which lay beneath the Saudi deserts. He agreed to supply the United States with oil to accelerate the industrialisation of the American economy.

The special US-Saudi relationship was formalised by Ibn Saud and President Franklin D. Roosevelt (b. 1882-d. 1945 CE) during their meeting on board the US naval ship USS Quincy in 1945 CE. This relationship was further strengthened after the Second World War when the oil demand increased phenomenally. It was also during this period that the United States became Saudi Arabia's most powerful political and economic ally. Thanks to the new petrodollars, the once backwards and poverty-stricken desert kingdom suddenly became one of the world's most prosperous countries. The credit for Saudi Arabia's transformation must go to Ibn Saud, who fought single-handedly for a quarter of a century to unify the warring Arab tribes and establish a State which is today considered to be one of the world's most affluent and influential countries.

Abd al-Aziz ibn Saud, the founder of the Kingdom of Saudi Arabia, eventually died at the age of seventy-five and was buried in his native Riyadh. He was succeeded by his eldest son, Saud. He ruled the kingdom for eleven years before abdicating in favour of his younger brother, Faisal. Like his father, Faisal was a wise and able ruler, but he was assassinated in 1975 CE. Khalid (b. 1913-d. 1982 CE), Ibn Saud's fourth son, then ascended the Saudi throne and ruled for seven years until he died in 1982 CE. He was succeeded by Fahd (b. 1921 or 1923 CE) who ruled the kingdom until he died in 2005 CE. Abdullah (b. 1924 CE), his half-brother, then succeeded him as King and he continued to serve in this capacity until he died in 2015 CE, when he was succeeded by Salman ibn Abd al-Aziz (b. 1935 CE), who is the oldest surviving son of Ibn Saud.

95

Muhammad Ali Jinnah (b.1876 - d.1948 CE) / (b.1293 – d 1368 AH)

The Mughal Empire was established in 1526 CE by Zahir al-Din Babar (Babur) and abolished by the British in 1857 CE. It was one of the foremost political dynasties to have ruled Muslim India. After more than three centuries of Mughal rule, the British arrived in India during the eighteenth century under the pretence of the East India Company and began to exert its influence in that country. As Mughal political authority rapidly weakened, the British tightened their grip on India during the first half of the nineteenth century and took full military control in 1857 CE. The establishment of British rule not only transformed the political and economic make-up of India, now its Muslim population also suddenly found themselves at the mercy of the British rulers.

The Muslims were once the masters of their own destiny but they now became the subjects of a foreign power. This naturally led to widespread discontent across India. However, the British imperial military operation suppressed all forms of rebellion. One such mass uprising took place in 1857 CE; better known as the Indian Mutiny. It thoroughly shook the Indian mind, body and politics and gave birth to the Indian liberation movement. It was led initially by the Muslims and later joined by the Hindus. The purpose of this public movement was to drive out the British from India. This movement soon gained momentum under the able leadership of many influential Indian Muslim leaders. They were instrumental in forcing the British to quit India. As a champion of the Indian liberation movement, Muhammad Ali Jinnah was a valiant fighter for the rights of Indian Muslims and the founder of Pakistan, now one of the world's most populous and powerful Muslim countries. He was undoubtedly one of the most influential Muslim political leaders of modern times.

Born in the historic Pakistani port city of Karachi, Jinnah's ancestors were originally Hindus, who originated from the Indian province of Gujarat, but it was his grandfather who embraced Islam. His father, Jinnahbhoy Poonja (b. 1855-d. 1931 CE), afterwards migrated from Gujarat and settled in Karachi where he became a moderately successful businessman. The modest income he generated from his business enabled him to send his young son to school, firstly in Karachi and then in Bombay (Mumbai). While he was still in high school, Jinnah married a local girl at the request of his parents. Thereafter, he sailed to England to study law. He arrived in London in 1892 CE and, although he did not like the English weather or climate, he soon settled down to his studies.

Tall, slim and unusually confident, Jinnah was very intelligent; indeed, he passed all his law exams with flying colours within two years. He was then called to the Bar at the Lincoln's Inn; he was only eighteen at the time. He was not known to have been an avid reader or a studious person, nevertheless, Jinnah's academic achievements were remarkable. During his stay in England, he developed a passion for politics and parliamentary debates. A staunch supporter of Dadabhai Naoroji (b. 1825-d. 1917 CE), the first Indian to be elected to the British Parliament, he assisted the Naoroji with his election campaign. After nearly four years in England, he returned to Karachi as a qualified barrister, only to discover that both his mother and young bride had passed away. Seeing his father struggling to make ends meet urged the young but ambitious Jinnah to sail to Bombay to seek legal work to support his poor family.

For the next three years, he was forced to endure considerable personal hardship and suffering as he struggled to find suitable employment. In 1900 CE, he was offered the available post of the Presidency Magistrate of Bombay. As a result, he was able to move into a better apartment and also bring his younger sister, Fatimah Jinnah (b. 1893-d. 1967 CE), from Karachi to Bombay to pursue her further education. Jinnah's relationship with Fatimah was a very special one. His six other siblings hardly feature in his long and distinguished life, whereas Fatimah became an integral part of his life. Indeed, she not only became his foremost supporter and advisor but also stood by him like a pillar throughout his life. As a talented lawyer, Jinnah pursued his legal duties with great skill, confidence and authority. He prepared his court cases with such care and thoroughness that, after entering the courtroom, he used to move around as if the case had already been won.

His confidence was disliked by his rivals, who accused him of cheekiness and arrogance, but Jinnah was neither arrogant nor cheeky. Rather he was an honest and bright lawyer who pursued his clients' cases as if they were his own. His clear and logical approach, coupled with his confident performance in court, often left his opponents spellbound. He became such a successful lawyer that his reputation soon spread in and around Bombay, which of course generated more work for him. During this period, he earned around five hundred rupees a day, which was significant pay and allowed him to lead a comfortable lifestyle. Also, being a Muslim member of the Hindu-dominated Indian National Congress, he increasingly became involved in the political affairs of his country.

If Jinnah was a talented lawyer, then he was an equally clever political operator who combined his role as an advocate (working for the British elites) and his nationalistic activities with remarkable success. Jinnah was keen to unite the Hindus and Muslims and work collectively to drive out the British from India. He attended the 1906 CE session of the Indian National Congress in Calcutta, where he acted as secretary to Dadabhai Naoroji, who was the president of the Congress at the time. Here he was acknowledged as 'the best ambassador of Hindu-Muslim unity' by Gopal Krishna Gokhale (b. 1866-d. 1015 CE), a prominent Hindu politician of the time. Jinnah's oratory skills, personal charisma and clear thinking were also widely admired by other prominent Hindus like Sarojini Naidu (b. 1879-d. 1949 CE), the acclaimed Indian literary figure.

During this period, he became a prominent defender of the rights and liberties of Indian Muslims, which made him very popular in the Muslim community. As his popularity continued to increase, he was elected president of the Lucknow Muslim League in 1916 CE, this further increased his political standing. Under Jinnah's guidance and stewardship, the Indian National Congress and the Muslim League signed the Lucknow Pact, and India's Hindus and Muslims became united for the first time. He was occupied with politics and his legal work and so had no time to marry again until he met young Ruttie Petit (b. 1900-d. 1929 CE), the daughter of a successful Indian businessman. This was a classic tale of love at first sight, and they married in 1918 CE. The atmosphere in Jinnah's Malabar Hill residence suddenly changed for the better, even if it was rather short-lived.

Until now Jinnah's entire political philosophy revolved around the notion of Hindu-Muslim unity and the need to liberate India from British political and military occupation. His political strategy worked well until Mohandas Gandhi (b. 1869-d. 1948 CE), better known as Mahatma Gandhi, left South Africa and moved to India during the 1920s. Gandhi was inspired by Hindu mysticism and he promoted a political philosophy which was radically different from that championed by Jinnah. It was expressed in the language of the Hindu religion. Gandhi's philosophy of non-violence soon captured the imagination of his Hindu followers, even if it did not go down too well with the Muslims.

As Gandhi gradually moved onto the centre stage of Indian politics under the banner of the Indian National Congress, Jinnah and the Muslim League became increasingly marginalised. To make matters worse, the ruling British elites also decided to side-step Jinnah (whom they considered to be a dangerous national-ist and a vocal opponent of their rule) in favour of a pacifist who preached non-violence. At the same time, his personal life was dev-astated when his wife, Ruttie, suddenly died in 1929 CE. Her death was a major blow to Jinnah, who promptly left Bombay for London where he lived with his daughter Dina and sister, Fatimah. Then Liaquat Ali Khan (b. 1896-d. 1951 CE), the future Prime Minister of Pakistan, visited him in 1934 CE and persuaded him to return to India to lead the Muslim League.

At the time, the League was suffering from a leadership crisis fol-lowing the death of prominent personalities like Hakim Ajmal Khan, Mawlana Muhammad Ali Jauhar and Sir Mian Muhammad Shafi. As a result, this powerful political body became rather ineffective.

The Indian Muslims, too, were crying out for a great leader to emerge and champion their cause. Jinnah became that saviour. The Jinnah-Liaquat partnership thus became one of the most decisive alliances to be formed in modern Indian political history.

Back in India, Jinnah energised the Muslim League which once more became a powerful force in Indian politics. And although increasing communal tension between the Muslims and Hindus threatened to split the country, Jinnah continued to advocate the need for understanding and cooperation between the two communities. It soon became clear that the supporters of Mahasabha wanted a free and liberated India to be shaped by no other ideology than their separatist and increasingly fundamentalist brand of Hinduism. So the Indian Muslims became alarmed. This also became a major cause of concern for Jinnah. So it was, between 1936 and 1937 CE, that one of the major turning points of his life took place. He exchanged several letters with Sir Muhammad Iqbal (see chapter 96), the influential Muslim poet-philosopher of India, who urged him to take a unilateral stand and fight for the rights of Indian Muslims.

Inspired by Iqbal's visionary call for a separate homeland for the Muslims of India, Jinnah now became an unrelenting champion of Pakistan. Thus, at the age of sixty, he not only reformulated his entire political philosophy, but also completely rearranged his whole outlook on life. Thereafter, the creation of a separate homeland for the Muslims of the subcontinent became his main occupation in life. Indeed, the decision of the Congress to declare Hindi to be the national language of a free, independent India, at the expense of other major Indian languages (such as Urdu), also prompted the Indian Muslims to demand a separate homeland for themselves. Following the Lahore Resolution in 1940 CE by the Indian Muslim leaders, led by A. K. Fazlul Huq (b. 1873-d. 1962 CE), the then Prime Minister of Bengal, Jinnah's quest for Pakistan moved a step closer.

After making a formal demand for the creation of a separate homeland for the Muslims of India, Jinnah travelled extensively across the country to mobilise support for his political project and unite the Indian Muslims under the banner of the League. During this period, he eloquently explained his vision of a new country where the Muslims of the subcontinent could live in peace and harmony. After a long and hard struggle, Jinnah's vision eventually became a reality in 1947 CE. A year after Pakistan appeared on the world map the inspirational *quaid-i-azam* (the great leader), as he now came to be known, died at the age of seventy-one and was buried in Karachi. Though Jinnah's vision for Pakistan was both bold and powerful, death intervened before he could translate his vision into reality. A man of his word, Jinnah always meant what he said. There is no doubt that he wanted Pakistan to be a model Muslim country: independent, strong, democratic, tolerant and wealthy — all underpinned by the universal values and ethos of Islam.

If Jinnah had lived for another five years, there is no doubt that he would have transformed Pakistan into an impressive political and economic power. Unfortunately for Pakistan, his great vision remains no more than a vision as successive Pakistani leaders failed to translate his vision into reality. Pakistan may be a great military power (it is the only Muslim country to have developed nuclear weapons capability), but its economy is in tatters. Likewise, more than forty per cent of Pakistanis are illiterate and the vast majority continue to live in abject poverty. In short, today's Pakistan is not the kind of Pakistan Jinnah had in mind; thus, the brave and visionary Jinnah must be figuratively turning in his grave.

Having said that, his vision for Pakistan is not dead. It is still alive and will continue to endure as long as Pakistan exists. As such, it is not impossible that a Jinnah-like leader may yet emerge in the future and realise his vision. If this were to happen, then his influence and legacy would no doubt become more widely recognised around the globe.

96

Sir Muhamamd Iqbal (b.1877 - d.1938 CE) / (b.1294 - d.1357 AH)

During the late nineteenth and early twentieth century, India produced some of the most influential Muslim leaders, thinkers and writers of the modern period. Not willing to live under British rule, the Indian Muslims led the Indian freedom movement. Thus, influential Muslim leaders like Mawlana Muhammad Ali Jauhar (b. 1878-d. 1931 CE) of the khilafat fame; A. K. Fazlul Haq (b. 1873-d. 1962 CE), better known as *sher-i bangla* (the 'tiger of Bengal'), and Muhammad Ali Jinnah, who became known as *quaid-i-azam* (the 'great leader') rallied the Muslim masses and urged them to free their country from foreign occupation. In so doing they left their permanent marks in the records of modern history.

Some celebrated Indian Muslim scholars and writers of the time included Allama Shibli Nu'mani, the famous author of *Sirat un-Nabi* (Biography of the Prophet); Sayyid Ameer Ali of Bengal, the celebrated jurist and popular author of The Spirit of Islam; Abdullah Yusuf Ali, the celebrated translator of the Qur'an into English, and last but not least, Mawlana Abul Kalam Azad, the towering Islamic intellectual and author of *Tarjuman al-Qur'an* (a commentary on the Qur'an). Sir Muhammad Iqbal, the hugely influential Muslim thinker and poet-philosopher of the subcontinent, belonged to this generation of outstanding Indian Muslims. His original poetic writings, coupled with his invaluable contribution to Islamic thought and philosophy, has today made him a household name, especially in Iran and the subcontinent.

Muhammad Iqbal's date of birth is debated by his biographers, either he was born in 1873, 1877 or 1896 CE. However, the majority say it was 1877 CE. His ancestors were Hindu Brahmins, who originally came from Kashmir and embraced Islam during the seventeenth century. Later, they left the Kashmir valley and settled in Sialkot in the Punjab. The city of Punjab is located between the historic cities of Lahore and Kashmir. Iqbal was born in Sialkot into a lower-middle-class Muslim family. His father Nur Muhammad was a tailor by profession. He was an illiterate Sufi who owned a small business but the modest income he generated from his business enabled him to lead a simple yet comfortable lifestyle.

Young Iqbal grew up under the watchful gaze of his devout father, who enrolled him at his local *maktab* (religious school) where he received elementary education in Persian, Arabic, Urdu and Islamic sciences under the guidance of Sayyid Mir Hasan. As an expert in Islamic sciences and classical Persian and Urdu literature,. Mir Hasan encouraged Iqbal to learn Persian and Urdu poetry. Thus, he read and learned to compose poetry while he was still in his teens. Iqbal was a bright student whose poetic imagination and ability impressed Mir Hasan, who encouraged him to enrol at the Scotch Mission School in Sialkot where he took his university entrance examination in 1893 CE.

When he was sixteen, Iqbal joined the Scotch Mission College (the present-day Murray College) and completed his intermediate studies. During this period, he married the daughter of a local physician and she bore him three children. At the age of about nineteen, he moved to Lahore and enrolled at the Government College. Here he studied Arabic, English literature and philosophy under the guidance of Sir Thomas Walker Arnold (b. 1864-d. 1930 CE), a distinguished British Orientalist and author of *The Preaching of Islam*, who encouraged him to pursue higher education. As a prominent scholar and historian of Islam, Sir Thomas was a lecturer at Aligarh's Muhammadan Anglo-Oriental College (MAO), today known as Aligarh Muslim University, where he collaborated closely with Allama Shibli Nu'mani before moving to Lahore. He was also well-known for his fair and sympathetic views about Islam.

Inspired by Sir Thomas's love of learning and scholarship, Iqbal hoped to pursue higher education in Europe to widen his intellectual horizons by acquiring first-hand knowledge of modern Western philosophy and sciences. After graduating with honours in Arabic and English literature, and also obtaining a master's degree in philosophy, he became a lecturer in Arabic at the Oriental College in Lahore. He was only twenty-three at the time.

During this period, he established his reputation as a gifted poet who could compose elegant and moving verses in Urdu. He regularly recited in front of large audiences in *musha'irahs* (poetic symposiums). Some distinguished Urdu poets of the time such as Nawab Mirza Khan Dagh and Mirza Arshad regarded Iqbal very highly. They encouraged him to compose more poetry. He pleased them by writing many poems on romantic, nationalistic, spiritual and emotional themes. The poems 'The Orphan's Cry', *Tarana-i-Milli* (National Anthem), and 'Picture of Grief' won him recognition throughout Lahore.

During this period, because he failed an exam in law he was unable to secure a civil service job due to medical reasons. But he did not lose hope and continued to teach at some of Lahore's leading institutions of higher education. He taught at the Government and Islamia Colleges. Following Sir Thomas W. Arnold's departure from Lahore for London in 1904 CE, Iqbal followed him and moved to England in 1905 CE.

He arrived in England at the age of twenty-eight and joined Trinity College, Cambridge. He attended James Ward and John McTaggart's lectures on philosophy. He worked closely with distinguished British Orientalists like Edward G. Browne and Reynold A. Nicholson. After obtaining a degree in philosophy, he moved to Munich University in Germany where he studied continental philosophy and wrote a doctoral thesis on the development of metaphysics in Persia. Thereafter, he returned to England where he was called to the Bar at Lincoln's Inn in London and qualified as a barrister. Iqbal's stay in Europe was, academically, a very successful period for him. It was also one of the most intellectually and spiritually defining moments of his life.

In Europe, he closely studied European philosophy and ideas. Iqbal observed Western culture and civilisation first-hand, but what he saw both shocked and surprised him. Full of life and vitality, he found the European people friendly, hardworking and studious. Thanks to their eagerness to study and explore the wonders of creation, a culture of learning and curiosity emerged in Europe. This enabled the Europeans to make great advances in philosophy, science and technology. By contrast, the Muslim world, which was once the pioneer of science, mathematics, philosophy, arts, culture and civilisation, now seemed to him to have become stuck in the past. The enthusiasm and energy of European civilisation compared with the unproductive and decadent condition of Islamic thought and culture was bound to shock and alarm a proud Muslim like Iqbal. He now began to explore his faith, its meaning and purpose in the modern world.

Iqbal had left India in 1905 CE as a young scholar, poet and nationalist, but his stay in Europe completely changed his view of Islam and its place and role in history. Living in an increasingly Western-dominated political, economic, educational and cultural landscape, he began to see his faith in a different light. Detached from the fantasy of the past, the nationalism of his own time and the money-oriented philosophies of the West, he explored European culture and the challenges which confronted the Muslim world then, in the light of the everlasting values of Islam. The results of his intellectual inquiry again shocked and disturbed him: if Western civilisation had made great progress in the fields of science and technology, it did not do the same in moral and spiritual advancement. This, in his opinion, did not mean progress or advancement. It was similar to building a castle on shifting sand; a disaster waiting to happen.

As for the Islamic world, although the Muslims possessed the final Divine revelation, he felt the Muslims had become occupied with the form rather than the spirit of the Divine scripture. This contributed to the gradual stagnation of the Muslim mind, thought, culture and civilisation. This analysis prompted him to explore ways in which he could renew the Muslim mind and thought and expose the dangers within scientific and cultural progress which lacked the moral and spiritual features of humanity.

After leaving London in 1908 CE, he returned home to India at the age of thirty-one and began to explore the problems and difficulties of modern civilisation in the light of Islamic values and principles. Like Malik ben Nabi (b. 1905-d. 1973 CE), the famous Algerian social scientist, and Sayyid Qutb (see chapter 102), the Egyptian Islamic thinker , Iqbal went to the West in search of knowledge and wisdom but returned home a strong and committed Muslim. He had discovered how weak the foundations of modern Western civilisation were and tried to reawaken his fellow Muslims from their sleep.

As a gifted poet and philosopher, Iqbal explained his ideas in his elegant and powerful poetry, which he wrote in both Urdu and Persian. He analysed and criticiszed modern philosophy and science through the philosophical lens of Islam. He attempted to revive Muslim thought and culture by creating a mixture between Islamic and modern Western thought, culture and values. The period from 1908 to 1936 CE was the most intellectually productive period of his life. As a qualified lawyer, he could have earned a very high salary and led a luxurious lifestyle, but instead, he chose to teach philosophy at the Government College in Lahore and practisce law on a part-time basis. This enabled him to earn enough to live comfortably and devote all his spare time and energy to developing his ideas and thoughts on how to reconstruct Islamic thought and refresh Muslim societies in the face of Western political, intellectual and cultural domination of the Islamic world.

Iqbal expanded his religious ideas and philosophical thoughts in many books of poetry published over more than thirty years. Thus, the *Shikwa* (Complaint) and *Jawab-i-Shikwa* (Response to Complaint) appeared in 1911 CE. They were followed by 'The Secrets of the Self'. Three years later, his 'The Mysteries of Selflessness' was published. Likewise, 'Message of the East', 'Gift of the Hijaz' and many others.

He was heavily influenced by the religious thoughts of Imam al-Ghazali (see chapter 56), and Jalal al-Din Rumi (see chapter 69), as well as the philosophical ideas of several European thinkers like Henri-Louis Bergson and Friedrich Nietzsche. Iqbal developed a powerful and dynamic philosophy which called on the Muslims to rise and boldly face the challenges posed by Western modernity, secularism and nationalism. His message was contained in poetic language and a degree of philosophical complexity. It was simple and effective. He urged the Muslims to take their destiny in their own hands by freeing themselves from European colonial rule and to rediscover the creativity and dynamism that is inherent in the meaning and message of Islam.

Iqbal made this point most eloquently in a series of lectures he delivered between 1928 and 1929 CE at the universities of Madras, Hyderabad and Mysore. These were later published as *The Reconstruction of Religious Thought in Islam* (1930 CE). In these lectures, he attempted to reformulate Islamic thought in the light of modern Western scientific and philosophical thought. He did so without completely breaking away from the traditional Islamic worldview. The lack of intellectual creativity, philosophical sophistication and cultural energy in the Muslim world had contributed, he felt, to the gradual decline of Islamic culture and civilisation. He therefore urged the Muslims to engage in a continuous process of *ijtihad* (exercise of individual judgement) to strengthen Islamic thought and culture.

If Iqbal was an outstanding Islamic thinker, then he was also one of the greatest Urdu poets since Mir Taqi Mir (1723 CE) and Mirza Asadullah Khan Ghalib (1797 CE). Far from being an intellectual loner, he encouraged Muslims to become activists and lead a vibrant life underpinned by Islamic morals and values. He practised what he preached and became actively involved in Indian politics. He served as a member of the Punjab Legislative Council. He was knighted in 1922 CE and became the president of the All-India Muslim League in 1930 CE. Thus, he occupied a prominent position in Indian public life. It was during his time as the president of the Muslim League that he developed the idea of creating a separate homeland for the Muslims of India.

In 1947 CE, Muhammad Ali Jinnah realised his vision in the form of the Islamic Republic of Pakistan. Iqbal did not live long enough to witness this momentous event. He died of illness at the age of sixty and was buried next to the famous Badshahi Mosque in Lahore. As the national poet of Pakistan and an influential Islamic thinker, Iqbal's poetry and message continue to inspire Muslims to this day; he is especially popular in Pakistan, Iran, India and Bangladesh.

97

Sa'id Nursi
(b.1877 - d.1960 CE) /
(b.1294 - d.1380 AH)

The decline of Ottoman political power in the face of a European attack on its territories in both Europe and the Middle East, combined with the rise of the Young Turks within the Ottoman state, encouraged Mustafa Kemal to rise to the challenge of defending mainland Turkey from European invasion. Mustafa was an ambitious Turkish military commander. After six hundred years of Ottoman rule, he sent the last Ottoman Caliph, Abd al-Majid II (b. 1868-d. 1944 CE), into exile in Switzerland. He then established the Turkish Republic in 1924 CE. He was considered as the saviour of Turkey. The honorific title of 'Ataturk' ('Father Turk') was later conferred on Mustafa Kemal for his personal bravery and military accomplishments. As the founder and undisputed leader of modern Turkey, he went out of his way to reform the political, educational and cultural institutions and practices of the Turkish people.

He was inspired by European Enlightenment ideas, thoughts and values. He attempted to change and reform Turkish culture and society in the light of modern European secular values and ethos. He distanced Turkey from its historical, cultural and linguistic links to the Islamic East to make Turkey an integral part of modern Europe. Turkey, he argued, belonged to Europe and thus he tried to thoroughly modernise and secularise Turkey. The majority of his people did not share his vision of the future. When the true colour of his social and cultural changes became clear for all to see, an influential Turkish Muslim thinker and reformer emerged to challenge Mustafa Kemal's secular crusade. This great Islamic scholar and reformer was none other than Sa'id Nursi, respectfully and fondly called Ustad.

'Bediuzzaman' (Wonder of the Age) Sa'id Nursi was born in the village of Nurs, in the eastern Turkish area of Bitlis. He was of Kurdish origin. His parents were devout Muslims who led a simple, religious and pious lifestyle. Ustad Sa'id began his education at home and learned the basics of Islam from his devout mother who inspired him to take a keen interest in religious matters. He became attracted to Sufism (Islamic spirituality) during his early years. The teachings of the famous Abd al-Qadir al-Jilani (see chapter 57) fascinated him the most. Indeed, his spiritual attachment to Shaykh al-Jilani grew stronger by the day. Later in life, he claimed to have been guided by this venerable Sufi Shaykh during some of the most difficult periods of his life.

His elder brother Abdullah encouraged him to join his village school when he was around nine. Blessed with a bright memory and a sharp intellect, he committed the entire Qur'an to memory with ease. His intellectual superiority over his fellow students, he later recalled, filled him with much pride and confidence. He enjoyed religious debate and discussion. His arrogant display of intellectual superiority often landed him in trouble.

However, after obtaining a diploma in Islamic sciences at the age of fourteen, he considered abandoning formal education for good. Thereafter, however, he claimed to have been visited by the Prophet Muhammad in the form of a dream. This prompted him to resume traditional Islamic sciences under the guidance of prominent teachers like Shaykh Mehmed Celali and Shaykh Mehmed Emin Efendi. After qualifying as an Islamic scholar, he moved to nearby Siirt where Shaykh Fetullah Efendi, a notable local scholar, gave him the title of 'Bediuzzaman' because of his vast learning and intelligence. When his popularity spread across Siirt, the local religious leaders reportedly became very jealous of him. He was forced to leave Siirt. He then travelled to other places where he faced similar opposition from local scholars on account of his great learning and matchless debating skills.

During his travels, he enhanced his reputation as a gifted scholar, skilled debater and accomplished athlete and warrior. Thanks to his unusual physical strength, he was able to run rings around his enemies and flee from danger on more than one occasion. At the time when Sa'id was busy pursuing his studies, the Ottoman State was passing through a period of considerable political uncertainty and cultural confusion. Once a great Islamic superpower, the Ottoman State was about to face a political and economic collapse in the face of Russian and Anglo-French attacks on its territories. Although Sultan Abd al-Hamid II (b. 1842-d.1918 CE) tried to stop the rot, his efforts proved futile as public dissatisfaction continued to spread across the country. This gave rise to the 'Young Turk' movement which, in turn, led to the removal of the Sultan from the Ottoman throne. The revolution of 1908 CE may have brought much-needed relief to the masses, but the Young Turks also failed to consolidate their grip on power.

During this chaos, Mustafa Kemal emerged to save his country from European invasion. The victory of 1922 CE confirmed his position as the founder of the new Turkish Republic. During this period of great political uncertainty, social unrest and economic suffering, Sa'id openly supported the reformists because he wanted his people's social and economic conditions to change for the better. But, he opposed the Young Turks' efforts to unite Islamic political theory with European constitutionalism. He considered their attempts to split education into three separate categories, namely religious (Islamic), spiritual (Sufi) and secular (modern), to be faulty from an Islamic perspective. Since his approach to Islam was a holistic and unified one, he felt the division of knowledge into such tight parts was unIslamic, unnecessary and counter-productive.

Indeed, after mastering the traditional Islamic sciences, he pursued advanced training in philosophy, spirituality, history, mathematics and the physical sciences. His exposure to modern sciences opened his mind to the dangers that were in modern Western secular ideas and thought. This prompted him not only to oppose the partitions of the Turkish educational system but also to urge the country's political and religious leaders to reform Turkey's traditional religious education curriculum. He proposed a new generation of Islamic scholars who could be trained to counter the challenges posed by modern Western atheistic philosophies and ideologies. During this period, he became actively involved in the social and political affairs of the state. He even participated in the war against the Russians on the Caucasian front. He was captured by the Russians and spent two years as a prisoner of war in Russia. He managed to escape in 1918 CE and returned to Istanbul, via Vienna.

Here he paid respect to Abu Ayyub al-Ansari, the famous *Sahabi* (companion) of the Prophet, who is buried in Istanbul. His spiritual retreat near the tomb of Abu Ayyub profoundly changed his outlook on life. He then carried out a detailed study of the Qur'an, the *Futuh al-Ghayb* (Disclosure of the Unseen) of Shaykh al-Jilani and the *Maktubat* (Letters) of Shaykh Sirhindi (see chapter 81). As a result, he claimed to have attained the height of Islamic spirituality. The 'Old Sa'id' became transformed into 'New Sa'id.

From then onwards, the Qur'an became his main source of guidance and spiritual illumination. He was a soldier who had fought bravely against the Russians in defence of the Turkish motherland. He also had mastery of Islam and aspects of modern sciences. Based on these two, it was clear that he could not be dismissed as a religious fanatic. In fact, he became a widely admired religious scholar. In 1923 CE Mustafa Kemal personally invited him to Ankara,; the capital of the new Turkish Republic, to officially recognise his contribution to the Turkish War of Independence.

But, on his arrival in Ankara, Ustad Sa'id was shocked by the culture of decadence which had gripped the capital during Ataturk's period. It was empty of tact, humility and gratitude. Mustafa Kemal and his juniors actively promoted a programme of Westernisation. Sa'id felt this was utterly inconsistent with the history, culture and ethos of the Turkish people and their faith. From Ankara, he retreated to Van where he engaged in meditation and spiritual exercises. His short visit to Ankara had confirmed his worst fears. The new Turkish rulers were no better than their predecessors. He considered Mustafa Kemal's eagerness to remove Islam from Turkish society by introducing Western-style reforms as both alarming and dangerous.

Ataturk abolished the Caliphate. He banned the traditional Turkish dress. He replaced the *hijri* calendar with the Gregorian one. He changed the Turkish traditional educational system in favour of a secular Western model. Mustafa Kemal was hoping to thoroughly undermine all major symbols of Turkey's Islamic past. However, the *ulama* (Islamic scholars) and the Sufis led a rebellion against his reforms. He responded by brutally suppressing his opponents. Sa'id became embroiled in this conflict even though he did not play a direct role in the uprising. However, as the Turkish authorities became suspicious of all the prominent religious scholars and Sufis, he was forced to flee to Western Anatolia.

Here he spent the next twenty-five years living in exile and travelling to many cities. During this period he found time to teach and train hundreds of students who later became prominent members of the *nurculuk* (the Nur movement). It was founded by Sa'id to preserve Turkey's glorious Islamic history, culture and heritage.

Even in exile, the Turkish authorities did not leave him alone. They continuously harassed, intimidated and persecuted him and his close associates. Later, he was arrested and charged with 'crimes' (such as writing disloyal books and supporting political opposition against the ruling regime, among other things). He was brought before the courts on more than one occasion, but he convincingly refuted all the charges levelled against him. During this period, he authored his *Risale-i Nur* (The Epistle of Light), a monumental commentary on the Qur'an of more than six thousand pages.

This work does not resemble a traditional *tafsir*. However, it is still considered to be one of the most influential Qur'anic commentaries of the twentieth century. In his book, he provided a systematic explanation of fundamental Islamic beliefs. He did this logically and scientifically. He felt such an approach to the Divine revelation was much needed in Turkey at the time because Western secular ideas began to gain the upper hand in that country. Since Sa'id considered Western philosophy to be purely rationalistic, and modern science to be entirely atheistic, he deliberately followed a logical, rational and scientific approach to the Qur'an to protect the Turkish people from the menace of Western atheistic thoughts. If Mustafa Kemal and his successors were eager to champion secular ideas under the disguise of progress, then Ustad Sa'id was determined to prove that the Qur'an was far from being out of date and backward.

On the contrary, the treasures of Islamic thought and culture were, in his opinion, far superior to Western thought and culture. This is because the Islamic worldview, unlike the Western materialistic worldview, was based on a holistic understanding of the whole of creation. This is where humans and nature are considered to be co-workers rather than as competing enemies. As expected, his intellectual attack on the Ataturk's secular idol made him an open target for the ruling party. They felt he was seeking to undo their entire programme of Westernisation and secularisation in Turkey. However, their harsh treatment of Sa'id only helped to strengthen his cause and his popularity began to spread throughout Turkey.

By the time of his death at the age of eighty-three, he had tens of thousands of followers across the country. Likewise, his *nurculuk* movement became a powerful force in Turkish society. Not surprisingly, his religious thoughts, as preserved in his monumental *Risale-i-Nur*, have become hugely popular in Turkey today. Also, eminent Islamic scholars and thinkers like Fethullah Gulen, Muhammad al-Buti, Necmettin Erbakan and Adnan Oktar, better known as Harun Yahya, have been deeply influenced by his religious thinking and Qur'anic scholarship.

98

Mustafa Kemal 'Ataturk'
(b.1881 - d.1938 CE) /
(b.1299 - d.1357 AH)

At its peak in the sixteenth century, the Ottoman Empire was one of the great political and military powers of the time. From Vienna in Europe to Yemen in the Arabian Peninsula, and from North Africa to Persia, the Ottomans ruled supreme in Europe, Asia and Africa. During this period influential Ottoman rulers like Muhammad (Fatih) II (see chapter 77) and Sulayman the Magnificent (see chapter 79) expanded the boundaries of their empire and promoted the arts, science and architecture throughout their dominion. In doing so, they radically transformed the fortunes of the Ottoman Empire.

The Ottomans were once a great political, economic and cultural power but they began to decline during the seventeenth century. However, while the visible signs of decline became clear for all to see, the ill-disciplined Ottoman rulers underestimated the seriousness of the situation which faced them. As the Ottoman Empire declined, the leading European powers began to spread their power. The Ottomans were faced with both internal decay and direct external threats from their European rivals. They were no longer in a position to hold their ground. Indeed, by the nineteenth century, the whole empire was now nearing total collapse. At this critical moment in Ottoman history, Mustafa Kemal, the founding father of modern Turkey and one of the most influential political leaders of modern times, emerged to save his motherland from total humiliation at the hands of its European rivals.

Better known by his honorific title Ataturk ('Father Turk'), Mustafa Kemal was born in Salonica (now Thessaloniki in Greece) into a lower middle-class Muslim family. His father, Ali Riza, was a junior civil servant who later became a relatively successful timber merchant. During his early years, Mustafa was enrolled at a Qur'anic school by his devout mother but he soon dropped out and joined a government-funded military school. Despite being brought up in a family where Islamic learning and education were highly valued, young Mustafa pursued a largely secular education. As a bright and confident student, he aspired to become a military officer rather than a religious instructor, as his mother wanted him to be.

Following the death of his father, the responsibility of looking after the family fell on the shoulders of his young mother. She was deeply religious and so encouraged her son to continue his studies. At the local military preparatory school, his teacher (who was also called Mustafa) added the word 'Kemal' to his name to distinguish the pupil from the teacher. From this time he became known as Mustafa Kemal. As a hardworking student, he excelled at school (especially in mathematics) and graduated in 1898 CE. He then enrolled at the War College in Istanbul at the age of eighteen.

At the War College, he worked extremely hard and combined his military education with nationalistic activities. He completed his studies at the age of twenty-one and was offered a place at the elite Staff College, where some of the country's brightest and most gifted students received advanced training in military tactics and strategy. Here at the Staff College, Mustafa and his associates became increasingly concerned by the internal problems which challenged Ottoman Turkish society at the time, not to mention the external threats it faced from the invading European powers.

Four years after completing his military training at the Staff College, he witnessed a mass uprising against the rule of Sultan Abd al-Hamid II (b. 1842-d. 1918 CE). This ended up as the revolution of the Young Turks in 1908 CE under the leadership of Major Enver Pasha. The Young Turks were led by a group of military officers.

They advocated the need for urgent political reform. They wanted an autocratic political system to become a parliamentary system of government so that political power could be exercised more efficiently and effectively, taking into consideration the external challenges which confronted the Ottoman State at the time.

The Young Turks' political aims and objectives were very relevant and commendable, but their understanding of both the internal and external challenges which threatened the Ottoman State was far too simplistic. They seriously underestimated the external threats the country faced at the time. This state of affairs angered and annoyed Mustafa who was then a member of the General Staff of the Officers' School in Salonica. So, he became very critical of the Young Turks' domestic and foreign policies. In truth, he felt the Young Turks were only making minor changes with the existing system rather than initiating bold and courageous political changes to stop the rot. Also, their close political and economic ties with Germany filled him with anger. As a proud Turk, he wanted the Ottomans to stand on their own two feet and set their house in order by themselves, without any foreign interference.

The Sultan's and the Young Turks' failure to start major reforms prompted Mustafa to promote his ideas on how to save the Ottoman State from total collapse. Then, in 1911 CE, the Italians launched a surprise military attack against the Ottoman province of Tripoli. Mustafa was keen to defend his country, so he took part in the campaign against the Italians, but harsh circumstances led to the Ottomans being forced to give up Libya to the Italians. As the Ottoman State faced serious external threats from prominent European nations, Major Enver Pasha invited the German army to come and help reorganise the Ottoman forces. Mustafa did not like this decision at all. He felt the Ottomans could do it without any foreign interference in their internal affairs.

To make matters worse, in 1914 CE the Ottomans entered the First World War on the side of Germany. This decision horrified Mustafa. As a gifted military strategist, he considered this decision to be deeply weak and predicted that it would have huge consequences for the Ottoman State. This is exactly what happened. Immediately after the war, the victorious European powers divided the Ottoman territories amongst themselves. During this critical time in Ottoman history, brave Mustafa fought forcefully to defend the Ottoman territories. After returning to Istanbul from the Arab front, he was shocked to discover how the British, Italian and French troops had forced the Young Turks to flee, before they marched into the Ottoman capital, – after smashing all Ottoman resistance.

To add insult to injury, the Allies then rewarded the Greeks, Turkey's bitter rivals, for entering the war on their side by giving them the city of Smyrna (present-day Izmir). When Mustafa was informed about this decision, he could no longer contain his rage. He was not prepared to allow the Greeks, their former subjects, to take control over an Ottoman territory. This would be a humiliation for the Turks. The proud Turks, he argued, could never accept such a proposition, let alone live under Greek rule. Not surprisingly, when the Greek troops landed in Smyrna, he ignored the Ottoman government and mobilised a resistance force to fight the Greeks. Ataturk had already acquired a reputation as an able military commander in 1915 CE when he successfully defended the Gallipoli Peninsula against the British. In that battle, he was rightly acknowledged by the Ottoman military for his heroic deeds at the time. But the challenge now presented by the Greeks in Smyrna was a totally different matter altogether.

The Turks in general, and Mustafa in particular, were determined to resist the Greek occupation. As an electrifying speaker and great motivator of people, he toured the local towns and villages and urged the masses to join his resistance movement. According to Mustafa, the purpose of this mass movement was to preserve Ottoman territorial integrity and re-establish an independent central government to reassert national independence and pride. When he asked the government in Istanbul to support his campaign, the authorities dismissed his suggestions and demanded that he return to Istanbul straightway. He refused to do so. Instead, he temporarily swapped his military uniform for civilian clothes. He then organised a secret conference at his base in the Kurdish province of Sivas. Here all the delegates, who arrived under the cover of darkness, collectively voted to form a rival government under Mustafa's leadership.

This marked the beginning of the end for the puppet government in Istanbul and showed Mustafa's emergence as a champion of the Turkish liberation movement. After he was elected head of a rival government, he cut off Istanbul from the rest of the country. This instantly isolated the existing government in Istanbul and forced Sultan Muhammad VI to sack his prime minister and order fresh elections in which Mustafa's supporters won a majority. The European powers, who had established their control across the Ottoman territories, were very alarmed. They began to closely monitor events as they unfolded in Istanbul. Frustrated by the central government's inability to return peace and order, the British army eventually marched into Istanbul in 1920 CE. The capital of the Ottoman State thus came under direct British military occupation.

A month later, Mustafa organized the first Grand National Assembly of Turkey in Ankara, where the delegates elected him as their President. In reality, he was only a president in name, for he had no political power, money or external support. Indeed, the Allies considered him and his supporters to be rebels who deserved to be captured and punished in an exemplary manner. But their failure to suppress the nationalistic feelings which now swept through Turkey eventually forced the Allies to call an urgent meeting in Paris to agree on the conditions of their withdrawal from Turkey. It was during this meeting that the Greeks were given the green light to invade Smyrna. The Greek invasion of this city further strengthened Mustafa's position and authority as a political leader and military commander. If the successful defence of the Gallipoli Peninsula increased his military standing, then Mustafa's remarkable achievement against the Greeks instantly turned him into a national hero.

At the decisive battle of Sakarya, in 1921 CE, a force of more than two hundred thousand unprepared and unequipped Turkish forces inflicted a crushing defeat on a quarter-of-a-million-strong Greek army. Under Mustafa's able leadership, the Turks hammered their Greek enemies and forced them to flee from Smyrna – leaving all their guns and weaponry behind. Victory on the battlefield consolidated his position as a famous leader of the Turkish people. The one-time Ottoman rebel now became the saviour of the Turkish motherland. After the Turkish liberation of Smyrna from the Greeks, Mustafa demanded that the Allies withdraw from Istanbul immediately. Thanks to his bravery and foresight, Turkey was not only saved from being divided by the Europeans, but his actions also prevented the destruction of six hundred years of Ottoman legacy, of which the Turks are very proud today.

As the leader of a free and independent Turkey, Mustafa began wide-ranging political, economic, and cultural changes in the country. He abolished the Ottoman Caliphate and transferred all political power to himself as the President of the Turkish Republic. He sent Abd al-Majid (b. 1868-d. 1944 CE), the last Ottoman Caliph, into exile to Switzerland in 1924 CE. A secular Turkish Republic thus appeared on the world map.

He was influenced by the ideas of European Enlightenment scholars, like Voltaire and Jean-Jacques Rousseau and so Mustafa wanted Turkey to be a modern, secular country like the other European nations. He was unable to reconcile Turkey's historical and cultural links to Islam with his aspirations to create a modern and secular nation. For this reason, he made wholesale political and cultural changes to promote his blurred and controversial vision of the future. He abolished the Turkish traditional clothing, including the fez. Much damage was caused to Islam and Muslim way of life. to He replaced the Islamic *hijri* calendar with the Gregorian one. He banned polygamy and the *hijab* (Islamic veil). He introduced the Latin script across Turkey. He also advocated equality between the sexes but failed to practise it himself.

Although he was brought up and educated in a devout Muslim family, he developed an unsympathetic attitude towards organised religion. Often, he showed his dislike of religious symbols and practices. Nevertheless, it is not possible to say categorically whether he ceased to be a Muslim, especially because he was very sympathetic towards Muslim nationalistic causes. For instance, he gave political refuge to the Sanusi Islamic leader against the Italians. He supported the translation of the Qur'an into Turkish for the benefit of those who did not understand Arabic. Yet, Mustafa's failure to accommodate Islam within his political and cultural framework left a huge question mark over his entire westernisation and modernisation programme in Turkey.

He was of course right to carry out the necessary social and political reforms to reduce mass poverty and illiteracy in Turkey, but his indiscriminate cultural reforms alienated his people whose attachment and loyalty to Islam he and his successors clearly underestimated. In other words, although Mustafa's remarkable contribution to the Turkish War of Liberation is acknowledged by all, his uncaring attitude to religion and wholesale cultural reforms have today made him a controversial figure, both within Turkey and across the Muslim world. Yet, no one can deny that he was one of the twentieth century's most influential political leaders, particularly for his impact on the development of the modern nation-state in the Muslim world. Ataturk's model of authoritarian secularism was followed by others including Reza Shah Pahlavi of Iran (r. 1926-1941 CE).

As far as the future of contemporary Turkey is concerned, there is no reason why Turkey cannot be a part of modern Europe, as Mustafa wanted it to be. But Turkey must first come to terms with its own historical and cultural self. Having been an Islamic superpower for six centuries, it cannot suddenly pretend to be an integral part of a secular and humanistic Europe. Rather it needs to reconcile its political, economic and cultural debt to Islam with its future hopes to be a part of the European Union. If it can achieve this balancing act, then Turkey can play an important strategic role in a constantly changing geo-political global order. A strong, tolerant, prosperous and Islamic Turkey can also play a pivotal role in bridging the gap between the Islamic world and the West.

This may not be what Mustafa wanted, but today we live in a completely different world. One that is dominated by information technology, regional politics, economic interdependence, cultural exchange, and international dialogue. Modern Turkey – founded and shaped by Mustafa – has the potential to become a major global power if it can reconcile its past with its present and thereby shape a bright future for itself.

Being a heavy drinker, Mustafa Kemal 'Ataturk' died of cirrhosis of the liver inside the Dolmabahce Palace at the age of fifty-seven and was buried in Ankara, the capital of modern Turkey. His admirers included British Prime Minister Winston Churchill, US President Franklin D. Roosevelt and the Indian Prime Minister Jawaharlal Nehru. Both Sir Muhammad Iqbal (see chapter 96) and Kazi Nazrul Islam (b. 1899-d. 1976 CE), the national poet of Bangladesh, wrote poems in his honour.

99

Muhammad Ilyas
(b.1885 - d.1944 CE) /
(b.1303 - d.1364 AH)

Muhammad ibn al-Qasim's arrival into the province of Sind at the beginning of the eighth century brought political Islam directly in contact with India. Unfortunately, his military excursion into India was brought to a sudden halt by the Umayyad Caliph Sulayman who recalled Muhammad ibn al-Qasim to Damascus following a family dispute. Although many Arab governors continued to rule Sind on behalf of the Umayyads and the Abbasids, it was Sultan Mahmud of Ghazna (see chapter 49) who picked up where Muhammad ibn al-Qasim left off and rapidly extended Islamic political and military rule into mainland India. As the Ghaznavids opened up India's political borders, Muslim traders and missionaries entered India in large numbers for commerce and the propagation of Islam. Led by the Sufi missionaries, Muslims poured into India and began to spread the good news of Islam throughout that country.

Thus influential Sufis like Abu Ali al-Sindi, Ali al-Hujwiri, Mu'in al-Din Chishti and Shaykh Ahmad Sirhindi (see chapter 81) became the pioneers of the Islamic mission on the subcontinent. Thanks to the efforts of these Sufi luminaries, large numbers of Hindus embraced Islam and, as a result, the message of Islam began to spread across India. As more and more Hindus entered the fold of Islam, the need for proper Islamic education and training became ever more important.

As expected, many Sufi groups filled this important gap by establishing *zawiyah* (khanqah or Sufi lodges) where the new converts received Islamic training and instruction. But despite the noble efforts of the Sufis, large numbers of Hindu converts went without any formal education or training in Islamic rites and rituals. Not surprisingly, therefore, many of these converts continued to lead a Hindu lifestyle while professing to be Muslims. This state of affairs continued in many parts of India until Muhammad Ilyas founded the *Tablighi Jama'at* (Organisation for Islamic Propagation) to address their religious needs.

Muhammad Ilyas, also known as Mawlana Ilyas, was born in Kandhla, near Delhi. His family were descendants of Shah Waliullah (see chapter 86), the great Indian Islamic thinker. Mawlana Muhammad Isma'il, the father of Ilyas, was a noted Islamic scholar who was heavily influenced by Sufi thought. He led a simple, austere lifestyle centred on devotional and preaching activities in his locality. After his father died, young Ilyas and his brother, Muhammad Yahya, were raised by their mother, Safia. As a *hafiza* (memoriser of the whole Qur'an), she ensured Ilyas also committed the whole Qur'an to memory. He then attended his local seminary to study Arabic and Islamic sciences. He then joined his older brother at Gangoh which was an important centre of Islamic learning and Sufism in India. Mawlana Rashid Ahmad Gangohi (b. 1826-d. 1905 CE) was a legendary Islamic scholar and Sufi of his time in Gangoh. Before he died in 1905 CE, Mawlana Gangohi personally initiated the twenty-year-old Ilyas into Sufism. During this period he completed his intermediate education and became an expert in Arabic, *tafsir* (Quranic commentary), *Hadith* (Prophetic traditions) and Sufism.

Despite suffering from poor health, Ilyas continued to pursue higher education in Islam and Sufism at Gangoh. His health problems frequently interrupted his advanced education until Mas'ud Ahmad, a local traditional physician and son of Mawlana Gangohi, diagnosed and treated him. Then, in 1908 CE, he enrolled at the famous *dar al-uloom* (Islamic seminary) in Deoband where he completed advanced training in *tafsir* and *Hadith* under *shaykh al-hind* Mawlana Mahmud Hasan (b. 1851-d. 1920 CE). He also received training in Sufism under the guidance of Mawlana Khalil Ahmad Saharanpuri (b. 1852-d. 1927 CE). Since Mawlana Gangohi was a mentor, spiritual guide and tutor of many renowned Indian scholars including Mawlana Ashraf Ali Thanvi and Mawlana Shah Abd al-Rahim Raipuri, Ilyas maintained close contact with these eminent scholars and personalities.

After qualifying as an Islamic scholar at the age of twenty-five, he began to teach at *mazahir ul-Islam* seminary in Saharanpur. As it was the annual *hajj* season, several local teachers decided to go to Makkah so the newly qualified Ilyas was offered a temporary teaching post. Two years later, he married the daughter of Mawlana Rauf al-Hasan. Some distinguished personalities like Mawlana Thanvi, Mawlana Raipuri and Mawlana Saharanpuri attended his marriage ceremony. Subsequently, in 1914 CE, he took leave from teaching and went to Makkah to perform the sacred *hajj* and resumed teaching on his return. In the same year, his brother and mentor, Mawlana Muhammad Yahya, suddenly died. His death profoundly affected Ilyas.

To make matters worse, two years later, his step-brother, Mawlana Muhammad, who at the time was in charge of the seminary founded by their father in Nizamuddin (near Delhi), also died from an illness. At the request of the locals, Ilyas left Kandhla and moved to Nizamuddin to take charge of this theological college. On his arrival, he found the seminary in a poor condition. Indeed, the lack of proper funding caused considerable hardship to all the teachers as well as the students. But, not afraid of the massive challenge he now faced, Ilyas reorganised the college and improved its academic performance. His new initiatives inspired the teachers and students alike, and the seminary began to thrive again.

During this period, Ilyas became aware of the dilemma of the Muslims of Mewat, located towards the southwest of Delhi. During the fourteenth century, the tribes of Mewat embraced Islam collectively. They were inspired by the great Indian Sufi sage Shaykh Nizam al-Din Awliyah (b. 1238-d. 1325 CE) and his disciples. But, deprived of proper Islamic education and training, they continued to live like Hindus while professing to be Muslims. Mawlana Ilyas was shocked and surprised by their political, social and economic condition and decided to take positive action to change and improve their lives. According to his biographers, he found the Meo people's religious, moral and ethical practices to be both mixed and confusing. Influenced by their Hindu past, the Muslims of Mewat freely partook in idol worship, celebrated Hindu festivals and engaged in many other un-Islamic activities. To outsiders, they appeared half-Hindu and half-Muslim.

To make matters worse, during the 1920s, the Meos became the target of several Hindu movements (such as the *Arya Samaj*) who attempted to re-convert these illiterate, tribal people to Hinduism. Since the majority of the Meo people were ignorant of Islam, the Hindus would probably not have faced much resistance from them. Characteristically, the Meos were very brave, hardworking and courageous people. It was their lack of Islamic knowledge and education which led them into a life of crime and banditry. Shocked by the awful condition of these people, Ilyas began to explore ways in which he could educate the Meos about their faith, culture and traditions. This, he felt, would enable them to lead better Islamic lives and improve their worldly condition.

After a period of reflection, he decided to proceed by promoting public education, although a severe shortage of Islamic schools in that region made his task very difficult. Undeterred by the lack of resources, he established his own religious seminary and began to train the local children in Islamic principles and practices so they could become ambassadors of Islam throughout the region. Initially, he encountered some resistance from the locals, who did not want their children to attend school. Being illiterate, these people failed to understand and appreciate the importance of educating their children. After some persuasion, Ilyas convinced them to allow their children to attend school at least for a part of the day.

Eventually, more and more locals allowed their children to attend school and, as a result, Islamic schools mushroomed throughout Mewat. For the first time in their history, the Meos actively encouraged their children to attend school and learn about their faith, culture and traditions. Funded partly by Ilyas and partly by local philanthropists, these schools and seminaries operated with minimal resources, but they managed to provide an acceptable level of Islamic education. Later, during one of his visits to Mewat, Ilyas noticed how the Islamic education provided by his schools failed to change and improve the local children's character, attitude and behaviour. He felt his attempts to reform Meo culture and society through the provision of free Islamic education were not achieving his aims and objectives. He therefore returned to the drawing board and explored other possible alternatives.

After due deliberation, he changed his strategy. That is to say, instead of pursuing a largely school-based educational strategy, he rolled out an informal educational programme aimed at changing people's behaviour and attitudes within their communities. In other words, he wanted to engage all the Meo people, children as well as adults, in the learning process through a mixture of school-based education and informal discussion and group work.

Mawlana Ilyas revealed that whilst in Madinah it was said to him that 'I shall take this work from you'. He did not know what this meant. Upon enquiry, a saintly person advised him not to worry about the kind of work to do as that would be taken care of by the One taking the service. On his return from his second *hajj* in 1925 CE, Ilyas recruited a number of local people and organised them into several groups. He then trained them in the fundamental principles and practices of Islam, before sending them off to their localities to preach Islam. The locals responded to the call of these Islamic workers with much interest and enthusiasm. He was convinced that he had discovered a workable *Tablighi* method. Ilyas then began to organise more *jama'at* (or a network of local Islamic workers) to carry out regular *Tabligh* missions in their towns and villages. During this period, he enlisted the support of all the major Islamic scholars of Mewat and rapidly expanded his religious activities across that region. The success of the *Tablighi Jama'at* enhanced his reputation as an eminent scholar and reformer of Islam.

Despite being occupied with the supervision and expansion of *Tablighi* activities, Ilyas found time to perform his third *hajj* in 1932 CE. On his return from Makkah, he began to establish *Tablighi* centres throughout Mewat, encouraging the local volunteers to focus their attention on the six points or principles of *Tablighi Jama'at*. These were *kalima/shahadah* (the declaration of faith); *namaz/salah* (five daily prayers); *ilm-o-dhikr* (seeking knowledge and engaging in meditation); *ikram-i-muslim* (serving and respecting fellow Muslims); *ikhlas-i-niyyat* (purifying intention), and finally *tafrigh-i-waqt* (volunteering for missionary activities). Learning and mastering these six points, argued Ilyas, was not an option but essential for all *Tabligh* workers because the attainment of personal purification, spiritual elevation, and good character and personality was the key to success in *da'wah* (invitation) work. In other words, according to Ilyas, to be a successful *Tabligh* worker one has to exemplify true Islamic qualities and attributes.

By combining the need for personal purity with the social and cultural reformation of society through mass volunteering and social activism, Ilyas initiated an Islamic movement which completely transformed the Mewat region. Indeed, his religious method proved so successful that over time the tablighi jama'at became one of India's most popular Islamic movements, even during his own lifetime. As an Islamic preacher and reformer, he deliberately refrained from political activism. Why? Because getting involved in politics, he felt, could distract him and his group of followers from their core objective to change, improve and strengthen people's faith, morals, character and personality. Later, accompanied by his fellow *Tablighi* leaders such as Mawlana Ihtisham ul-Hasan, Mawlana Muhammad Yusuf (b. 1917-d. 1965 CE) and Mawlana Inam ul-Hasan (b. 1918-d. 1995 CE), Ilyas performed his fourth and last pilgrimage in 1938 CE. Six years later, he died at the age of fifty-nine and was buried in Nizamuddin.

The Islamic movement he founded continued to prosper under the able leadership of his son, Mawlana Muhammad Yusuf. He became known to his followers as *'hazrat-ji'* (His Excellency). He went out of his way to tour the entire subcontinent to promote the work of *Tablighi Jama'at*. Thus, new *Tablighi* centres mushroomed in both East and West Pakistan. Subsequently, under the leadership of Mawlana Inam ul-Hasan, *Tablighi Jama'at* spread across the world including Southeast Asia, Africa, Europe, as well as the Americas.

As a staunchly apolitical religious movement, *Tablighi Jama'at* has been able to operate freely both in the Muslim world and the West, unlike, for instance, the more politically active Islamic organisations like *ikhwan al-muslimun* (The Muslim Brotherhood) in the Arab world or the *jama'at-i-islami* (The Islamic Organisation) in the subcontinent. With its headquarters still based at Nizamuddin, today the *Tablighi Jama'at* has become one of the most influential and widely followed Islamic movements of all time, with millions of followers across the world.

100

Ayatullah Khomeini
(b.1902 - d.1989 CE) /
(b.1312 - d.1410 AH)

The word 'Iranian' (meaning 'from the land of the Aryans') referred to those people who had migrated to the Iranian plateau around 1500 BC. Over time, they became known as the 'Persians'. However, the Shah of Iran officially banned this term in 1935 CE. Historically speaking, after the collapse of the ancient Persian Empire around 331 CE, the Iranian territories were taken up by the Macedonians, Seleucids and Parthians until the Muslims emerged from Arabia and conquered Iran in 641 CE during the reign of Caliph Umar (see chapter 6). With the advent of Islam, the Iranian people embraced the religion of their conquerors and contributed immensely to the development of Islam as a religion, culture and civilisation. With the decline of the once-mighty Abbasid Empire, there then emerged many independent dynasties in the Muslim world such as the Seljuks, Mongols and Timurids.

They ruled the Iranian people until the Safavids. They were a local Iranian dynasty which emerged at the beginning of the sixteenth century. They ruled for more than two hundred years before the invading Afghans destroyed them in 1722 CE. Thereafter, Iran became a playground for the Turks, Russians and the British. They fought each other to control the country until, in 1906 CE, an independent constitutional monarchy was established in Iran. This lasted until the Iranian Revolution of 1979 CE erupted and completely transformed the political map of that part of the world. The father of this revolution was Ayatullah Khomeini. He is one of modern history's most influential political and religious figures, who single-handedly brought down the Shah of Iran and established an Islamic theocracy which today plays a significant role in world politics.

Ayatullah Ruhullah Khomeini, known as Imam Khomeini for short, was born in Khomein, a small village in Central Iran located about two hundred miles south of Tehran, the capital of Iran. His ancestors claimed to be descendants of the Prophet, through Musa ibn Ja'far al-Kadhim (b. 745-d. 799 CE), the seventh Shi'a Imam. After settling in Nishapur, they migrated to India at the beginning of the eighteenth century. In India, Khomeini's immediate ancestors settled in Kintur, near the Indian city of Lucknow, where his grandfather Sayyid Ahmad Musavi was born and raised. Later, he moved to Najaf, the famous Iraqi shrine city, in around 1830 CE to pursue higher education. After completing his education, he decided not to return to India. Instead, he settled in Khomein, married thrice and became a successful entrepreneur.

His father, Mustafa, was born in 1856 CE and became a respected Shi'a cleric but he was murdered during a local dispute. Khomeini was only around five months old at the time. He was Raised by his mother and uncle Sayyid Murtaza Musavi. Young Khomeini grew up to be a talented student and a keen sportsman. Having inherited a sizeable plot of land and a few small businesses from his father, his mother was able to pay for his education and ensure the family also lived quite comfortably.

He completed his early education in Arabic, Persian, Shi'ite theology, literature and poetry at his local village school. Then, at the age of seventeen, Khomeini moved to a place called Arak where Shaykh Abd al-Karim (b. 1859-d. 1937 CE), an important Shi'a scholar had founded a theological seminary. He enrolled at this institution for further education. Here he studied Arabic grammar, literature and the religious sciences before moving to Qom, a famous centre of Shi'a learning and scholarship in Iran.

In Qom, Khomeini devoted all his time and energy to his studies, swiftly mastering the standard texts in *fiqh* (Islamic jurisprudence), *tafsir* (Quranic commentary), *Hadith* (Prophetic traditions), *ilm al-kalam* (scholastic theology) as well as logic and ethics under the guidance of prominent Shi'a luminaries of the time. Although Khomeini was a bright student of the *zahiri* (external) sciences of Islam, he also became fascinated by poetry, *tasawwuf* (spirituality) and Shi'a *batini* (inner) knowledge.

Accordingly, he carried out an extensive study of *hikmat* (traditional philosophical) and *irfan* (gnostic) sciences – as originally developed by Ibn Sina (see chapter 52), Suhrawardi (see chapter 64), Ibn al-Arabi, (see chapter 65), al-Tusi (see chapter 68), Mulla Sadra (see chapter 82) and others. He did so under the instruction of eminent teachers like Mirza Ali Akbar (b. 1851-d. 1926 CE) and Mirza Muhammad Ali Shahabadi (b. 1875-d. 1950 CE).

Being very fond of mystical poetry, he studied and the works of Hafiz of Shiraz (b. 1315-d. 1390 CE), Umar Khayyam (see chapter 55) and the celebrated *Mathnavi* of Jalal al-Din Rumi (see chapter 69). Khomeini's mastery of both the *exoteric zahiri* (external) and *batini* (external) Shi'a teachings was acknowledged by his tutors who formally awarded him a diploma in traditional Islamic sciences. He rapidly acquired a reputation as a promising young scholar and practitioner of Sufism. Of all his teachers, it was Shahabadi who profoundly influenced Khomeini's ideas and thoughts on philosophy, ethics, morality and politics. Shahabadi emphasised the importance of leading a scrupulously clean, pious and austere lifestyle.

Unlike the majority of the Shi'a clerics and mystics of the time, he urged his students to become intellectually and politically active. Indeed, he argued, it was the religious obligation of all Muslims, scholars and lay people alike, to oppose the anti-Islamic, oppressive and unjust policies of the Shah. His social and political interpretation of Shi'a theology and philosophy inspired Khomeini and later provided him with the religious justification for starting his political campaign against the Shah.

After completing his formal education in Qom, Khomeini started lecturing there while he was still in his late twenties. At the time, serious social and political changes were taking place across Iran. Khomeini was aware of the challenges facing the Iranian people. The rise of Reza Shah Pahlavi (b. 1878-d. 1944 CE), and the founding of the Pahlavi dynasty during the 1920s, raised the hopes and aspirations of the Iranian people. Soon after gaining power, the

Shah initiated wide-ranging legal and administrative reforms. He also constructed new roads and railways. He established schools and colleges. He attempted to modernise Iran's towns and cities – as well as industrialise its economy – along the European lines. Following in the footsteps of Mustafa Kemal 'Ataturk' of Turkey (see chapter 98), the Shah was determined to Westernise Iran by force, if necessary.

However, his failure to merge modern Western secular values with the deeply rooted Islamic culture and traditions of Iranian society was destined to create much opposition within the country. As a teacher and Shi'a cleric, Khomeini observed the events which unfolded in Iran at the time with great concern. During this period, he authored his *Kashf al-Asrar* (The Disclosure of Secrets). In it, he severely criticised and attacked the Shah for presiding over a corrupt gGovernment and for punishing and humiliating the Shi'a luminaries. In so doing, he formulated his views on Islam and political governance for the first time.

If Reza Shah's maltreatment of his opponents served as a wake-up call for Khomeini, then it was the failure of his successor, Muhammad Reza Shah Pahlavi (b. 1919-d. 1980), to learn lessons from his father's mistakes which forced Khomeini to engage in political activism. Like his father, the new ruler was determined to Westernise Iran. Despite protests from the country's religious scholars, the Shah tried to change the social and cultural values and practices of the Iranian people. But the masses – inspired by the powerful Shi'a clergy – rejected such wholesale change and reformation. This led to violent clashes between the clergy with the masses against the Shah's security forces. Now increasingly recognised as a powerful religious figure in Qom and thanks to the popularity of his lectures on Shi'a theology, philosophy and ethics, Khomeini began to openly criticise the Shah's regime for its heavy-handed tactics and autocratic policies.

As soon as he began to urge the masses to stand up against the Shah and oppose his anti-Islamic policies, Khomeini was arrested and imprisoned by the regime in 1963 CE. But his spell in prison only helped to establish his reputation as a champion of the Iranian people. His rising popularity eventually forced the Shah to release him a year later. Soon afterwards he once again annoyed the authorities by speaking out against American interference in Iran's internal affairs. As a result, the Shah re-arrested Khomeini and in 1964 CE exiled him to Turkey.

He spent the next fourteen years in exile in Turkey, Iraq and France. During this period, he maintained close links with his supporters back in Iran. After establishing contacts with various Iranian opposition groups in Europe and America, he openly called on the Iranian people to rise against the Shah and his cohorts. His long stay in the Iraqi city of Najaf, a prominent centre of Shi'a religious learning and scholarship, was a critical period for Khomeini. Here he gathered around him a group of followers who supported his efforts to overthrow the tyrannical Shah and install an Islamic Government in Iran. The Shah, argued Khomieni, despised the clergy more than any other sector of Iranian society because they opposed his wholesale reformation of the country's educational, cultural and religious institutions, and for openly rejecting his attempts to Westernise Iranian culture and society

But Khomeini and his supporters were determined not to allow the Shah to succeed. Even Western-educated Iranian scholars and intellectuals became involved in this debate. Indeed, some of them argued that it would be disastrous for Iran to adopt Western secular values at the expense of its traditional Islamic culture and norms. The pro-Islamic views of intellectuals like Ali Shari'ati and Murtaza Mutahhari also encouraged the Iranian people to join the growing Islamic movement in the country.

As the voices of Islam began to multiply, the Shah appeared to be fighting a losing battle. Khomeini delivered a series of lectures in Najaf in 1969 CE in which he formulated his concept of an Islamic government for the first time. Later published as *Vilayat-i-Faqih: Hukumat-i Islami* (The Vice-Regency of the Jurist: The Islamic Polity), in this book he developed a design for an Islamic Republic in Iran. He argued that it was the duty of every Muslim, cleric or layman, to work collectively to establish an Islamic Republic in Iran along the lines of the seventh-century Madinian model. He urged religious scholars to reclaim their role as heirs of the Prophet and assume the social and political leadership of their society.

Khomeini's concept of *vilayat-i faqih* was both innovative and powerful. He argued that in the absence of the *Ghayba* (Hidden Imam), those who possessed a sound knowledge of Islamic law and jurisprudence had no choice but to assume the political and religious leadership of the country. This, therefore, provided him with the religious justification for the rule of the clerics following the Iranian Revolution of 1979 CE. Having said that, Khomeini's social and political reading of Shi'a theology and jurisprudence was vigorously opposed by scores of influential Shi'a luminaries such as al-Khoi, Shariatmadari and Sistani. However, he simply ignored them – as did the majority of the Iranian people.

Thereafter, he published his *Jihad-i Akbar* (The Greater Struggle) in which Khomeini argued that the clerics and the public should spiritually cleanse themselves through regular prayers and fasting which, in his opinion, was an essential pre-requisite for the attainment of success in this world and the hereafter. It was during his time in exile that he developed his ideas and thoughts on political governance, social philosophy, Islamic morality and ethics. While he was busy working on a feasible Islamic political system, the Shah's grip on power began to weaken. Indeed, as mass protest against his autocratic rule gathered pace in 1978 CE, Khomeini, who was then living in exile in Paris, urged his supporters to continue their political campaign until the Pahlavis were ousted from power.

During this momentous period in modern Iranian history, Khomeini became a powerful symbol of resistance and hope for millions of Iranian people across the world. It was also during this period that much discussion and debate raged in Iran concerning the country's future direction. One group, led by Mehdi Bazargan (b. 1907-d. 1995 CE) the eminent leader of the Iran Freedom Movement, advocated the need for a gradualist approach to social and political change because they wanted to establish a moderate Islamic government in Iran. But their voices were drowned out by the supporters of Khomeini, who opted for a strict, hard-line and clergy-dominated political administration in Tehran. Surrounded by his close associates and supporters like Mutahhari, Beheshti, Rafsanjani and Ali Khamene'i, a triumphant Khomeini returned to Tehran and announced the establishment of the Islamic Republic in 1979 CE.

This marked the end of more than fifty years of Pahlavi rule, and the beginning of a new chapter in Iranian history. Khomeini ruled Iran for more than a decade and tried to address its internal, as well as external, threats and challenges with great resolve and determination. But the tussle between the advocates of moderation and Islamic liberalism on the one hand, and the advocates of traditionalism and religious literalism on the other continues to this day. Although it is not clear which of these two powerful religious factions will have the final say about the future direction of their country, there is no doubt that Khomeini's legacy will play a powerful role in Iranian politics, at least for the foreseeable future. Ayatullah Khomeini died at the age of around eighty-seven and was buried in the famous cemetery of Behesht-i Zahra in Tehran.

101

Abul A'la Mawdudi (b.1903 - d.1979 CE) / (b.1313 - d.1400 AH)

If the nineteenth century was the age of European domination of the Muslim world, then the twentieth century must be considered the period when the Muslims finally woke from their sleep and began to liberate their lands from foreign occupation. At the height of European colonisation, Muslim leaders and the people channelled all their energy in one direction, namely the liberation of their countries from European colonial rule. But following the departure of the British, French, Italians and the other European colonial powers from the Muslim world, a powerful and pertinent debate took place in all the Muslim countries concerning their political and constitutional futures.

The secular, liberal Muslim political elites favoured a Western-style political and constitutional arrangement. Others, on the other hand, argued that a socialist model of political governance and economic management was a more suitable option. The Islamists championed the need for a political framework based on their understanding and explanation of Islamic principles. After decades, if not centuries, of European political and economic domination, the debate concerning the future direction of Muslim countries raged across the Islamic world. It provided a perfect opportunity for Muslims to develop a system of political governance and economic management based on Islamic principles and practices. One Islamic scholar and activist contributed more to this debate than probably any other Muslim thinker or reformer of his generation. He was Abul A'la Mawdudi of Pakistan.

Sayyid Abul A'la Mawdudi, better known as Mawlana Mawdudi, was born in the town of Aurangabad in the Indian State of Hyderabad (in present-day Andhra Pradesh). His father, Sayyid Ahmad Hasan, was a lawyer by profession, who claimed to be a descendant of the Prophet through a chain of Indian Sufi luminaries connected to the famous *chishtiyah* Sufi Order. Young Mawdudi was born and brought up in a family where learning, personal piety and devotion to Sufism were valued and respected. He received his early education at home from his father. When he reached school age, he enrolled at *madrasah al-fawqaniyah*, a local seminary, to pursue traditional religious education.

Sayyid Ahmad Hasan himself received a Western education at the Muhammadan Anglo-Oriental College (present-day Aligarh Muslim University), founded by Sir Sayyid Ahmed Khan in 1875 CE. He qualified as a lawyer but encouraged his young son to become an *alim* (traditional Islamic scholar). As a bright student, Mawdudi completed his studies at *madrasah al-fawqaniyah* before joining the *dar al-uloom*, an Islamic college, in Hyderabad for further education in Urdu, Arabic and traditional Islamic sciences. But his further education was interrupted at the age of seventeen when his father died. Sayyid Ahmad Hasan's spiritual tendencies, coupled with his ascetic ways, contributed to his family's economic difficulties. After his father's death, Mawdudi was forced to abandon his studies and work to earn a living.

According to Mawdudi's biographers, he acquired a powerful command of Urdu and Arabic and became sufficiently familiar with traditional Islamic sciences to continue his study and research. At the same time, he began to write articles and essays on different aspects of Islam with unusual clarity and vision. His knowledge of current affairs – and his awareness and understanding of the problems which confronted the Indian Muslims at the time – enabled him to secure the editorship of a local Muslim newspaper.

He then became editor of the more prominent *al-Jam'iyat*, the official publication of Jam'iat-i Ulama-i Hind, a national Islamic umbrella organisation, which represented the Indian Muslims at the time. His time as editor of these publications enabled Mawdudi to polish his writing skills, earn a decent income and also acquire a better understanding of Indian politics and public affairs. During this period, he also composed scores of articles wherein he defined the Islamic concept of *jihad* (personal and collective struggle) to clarify existing misconceptions about this important Islamic obligation. These articles were later published under the title of *al-Jihad fi'l Islam* (War and Peace in Islam).

Following his resignation as editor of *al-Jam'iyat* in 1928 CE, Mawdudi left Delhi and moved to Hyderabad. He continued his literary activities, writing and translating books from both Arabic and Persian into Urdu under the supervision of outstanding Islamic scholars like Abd al-Majid Daryabadi (b. 1892-d. 1977 CE) and Sayyid Manazir Ahsan Gilani (b. 1892-d. 1956 CE). During this period, he also composed his *Risalat-i Diniyat* (Towards Understanding Islam), a small but popular booklet on fundamental Islamic beliefs and practices.

By the time Mawdudi had completed this book in 1932 CE, his understanding of, and approach to, Islam had shifted considerably. As a journalist and editor of *al-Jam'iyat*, he was clean-shaven and wore Western clothes, but now he grew a beard and adopted a revivalist approach to Islam. He was convinced that the Indian Muslims were facing considerable political challenges from the British elites as well as the Hindu public. He responded to the ever-changing social and political situation by promoting Islamic knowledge and raising awareness of Indian political affairs.

With this in mind, he took charge of *Tarjuman al-Qur'an* (Interpretation of the Qur'an) in 1932 CE. This was a monthly Islamic journal which was originally published by an independent Muslim scholar in Hyderabad. Through this journal, Mawdudi established himself as a leading advocate of Islam in India. As a prolific writer, he contributed most of the articles in the journal and his concise, relevant and refreshing approach to Islamic political, legal and social issues. It instantly won him much praise from other renowned Indian Islamic scholars and thinkers like Sir Muhammad Iqbal (see chapter 96), Sayyid Sulayman Nadwi (b. 1884-d. 1853 CE), Mufti Muhammad Kifayatullah (b. 1875-d. 1952 CE) and Sayyid Manazir Ahsan Gilani. This convinced Mawdudi that his intellectual efforts were having the desired effect and thus he continued to champion the cause of the Indian Muslims and write abundantly.

Mawdudi continued to publish the *Tarjuman* from Hyderabad until 1937 CE. Then Sir Muhammad Iqbal invited him to move to Pathankot (located in East Punjab, India) and help him to establish an Islamic research centre there. After his move to Pathankot in 1938 CE, he continued to edit and publish the *Tarjuman* and also began work on the proposed research centre. With the assistance of some of India's prominent Islamic scholars, he eventually established the centre and began to supervise its activities, and in his spare time, he continued to write productively on all aspects of Islam. However, over time he felt that conducting research and writing books alone was unlikely to lead to political reform and social change. Rather a combination of social and political activism, reinforced by the permanent values and principles of Islam, was more likely to bring about such change.

With the active support of many leading Indian Islamic scholars, in 1941 CE he formally launched the *jama'at-i-islami* (The Islamic Organisation), an Islamic political party, to reform Indian politics, culture and society in the light of Islam. As an Islamic scholar and writer, Mawdudi's monthly articles in the *Tarjuman*, coupled with his books, soon captured the imagination of both traditional Islamic scholars as well as modern, educated Indian Muslims. However, as the founder and *ameer* (chief) of *jama'at-i-islami*, he was still a marginal political figure. However, this situation changed radically following the formation of Pakistan as an independent country in 1947 CE. Along with his close friends and supporters, Mawdudi left India in favour of Pakistan and tried to establish an Islamic political, economic and cultural order there.

The *Tarjuman* became the chief journal for the explanation and propagation of his political and religious thoughts. But it was the formation of *jama'at-i-islami* in 1941 CE — and his subsequent migration to Pakistan in 1947 CE — which provided the ideal opportunity for him to engage in politics on a full-time basis for the first time. Before he arrived in Pakistan, Mawdudi was known primarily as an Islamic scholar and writer, and his *jama'at-i-islami* was viewed as yet another religious organisation. However, after his move to Pakistan, he became an active politician. The *jama'at-i-islami* also became known as a political party which actively campaigned for an Islamic constitution, as well as the need to implement the *Sharia* (Islamic law) in that country.

During this period Mawdudi wrote prolifically on Islamic political, legal and constitutional matters. He was hoping to influence both the politicians and the masses in the devising and implementation of a system of political governance, economic policies and legal framework which was compatible with Islamic principles and values. Mawdudi did not believe in the pursuit of intellectual activity minus social and political activism. Indeed, influenced by the reformist ideas of prominent Islamic thinkers like Ibn Taymiyyah (see chapter 72), Shaykh Ahmad Sirhindi (see chapter 81), Shah Waliullah (see chapter 86) and Sir Muhammad Iqbal, Mawdudi combined theology with politics, spirituality with social activism and philosophy with the need for cultural renewal. And although his political activism landed him in prison several times, he remained as steadfast as ever.

Mawdudi argued that Islam in its broadest sense was an all-inclusive religion and ideology. Thus, there was no room for the compartmentalisation of politics from Islam, economics from justice, and freedom from responsibility. Rather, he considered Islamic teachings to be holistic and all-encompassing, covering all aspects of human life in a structurally inter-connected and interdependent way. It radiated from one Divinely inspired source, namely the Qur'an, and the authentic Sunnah (practice of the Prophet). Thus, he believed, there was no room for separating politics from Islam.

Accordingly, Mawdudi and his *jama'at-i-islami* fully embraced social and political activism. Indeed, they believed this to be one of the most effective ways to bring about political change and social reform in Muslim societies, especially at a time when the rulers deliberately chose to sideline or undermine Islamic principles concerning political governance, economic management, educational policy, social justice, law and order, and cultural development and social morality.

As an Islamic thinker and author, Mawdudi wrote more than one hundred books on all aspects of Islam. His exposition of Islam as a religion and complete way of life was always clear and comprehensive. Some of his most important books were 'Collection of Lectures', 'A History of Islamic Revivalist Movements', 'Usury', 'The Veil', 'The Islamic Way of Life' and 'The Islamic Political Theory'.

However, it is his *Tafhim al-Qur'an* (Towards Understanding the Qur'an), a voluminous Urdu translation and commentary on the Qur'an, which is today considered to be his most influential work. In this vast and unusual commentary, written over a period of thirty years and published in six hefty volumes, he tried to explain the reason for the Qur'anic revelation clearly and logically. As a politician and activist, Mawdudi tried to highlight the fundamental teachings of the Qur'an for the benefit of scholars as well as lay people. He also went out of his way to explain how one could translate the message of the Qur'an into one's daily life.

Mawdudi was not interested in intellectual discussion or debate for its own sake. Rather he was motivated by the desire to reform Muslim societies in the image of the Divine message, and in so doing he hoped to improve people's quality of life. The *Tafhim* is a popular Qur'anic commentary, having been translated into multiple languages. It has also been translated into English consisting of fourteen volumes.

However, according to some of Mawdudi's critics, he emphasised the social and political dimension of Islam at the expense of its moral and spiritual dimensions. That is to say, his critics have argued that his books read more like manuals for social and political action, rather than works of Islamic wisdom and spirituality. In the final analysis, however, Mawdudi was more successful as a writer and Islamic scholar than he was as a politician and activist. But the *jama'at-i-islami* party which he founded and led for more than three decades continues to operate in Pakistan, India, Bangladesh and Sri Lanka to this day. Though the party has not been as successful as Mawdudi and his associates had anticipated, its influence is still quite considerable in the subcontinent.

By contrast, Mawdudi's writings have been translated and published in all the major languages of the world. He is today considered to be one of the most widely-read Muslim authors of modern times. He died in a hospital in Buffalo (New York) at the age of seventy-five and was buried in front of his house in Lahore. Before his death, Mawdudi received the prestigious King Faisal International Award for his services to Islam. Likewise, his religious thoughts have influenced scores of prominent modern Muslim scholars including Sayyid Qutb, Muhammad al-Ghazali, Abul Hasan Ali Nadwi, Muhammad Manzur Nu'mani, Amin Ahsan Islahi, Israr Ahmad Wahiduddin Khan and Khurshid Ahmad among others.

102

Sayyid Qutb
(b.1906 - d.1966 CE) /
(b.1324 - d.1386 AH)

As representatives of the Ottomans, the Muhammad Ali Pasha (b. 1769-d. 1849 CE) dynasty ruled Egypt for more than half a century before the British occupied it in 1882 CE. Being proud Muslims, the Egyptians intensely disliked foreign military occupation of their country. However, the nineteenth century represented an unstable period in Egyptian (and Islamic) history for two important reasons. Firstly, during this period a large part of the Muslim world was colonised by the leading European nations, who undermined the political and economic infrastructure of the Muslim countries. Secondly, the invasion of European culture and values into the Muslim world led to considerable social and cultural tension and confusion. As political instability and social unrest gripped much of the Muslim world, several powerful local nationalist movements emerged to challenge the occupying forces.

In Egypt, the spread of nationalist passion during the early part of the twentieth century forced the British to grant formal independence to Egypt. Although the Egyptian nationalists, like others in many different parts of the Muslim world, fought vigorously to liberate their country, they failed to prepare for the aftermath. This proved particularly disastrous for Egypt, as rival political groups proposed competing visions for the future of the country. Some supported a secular, European-style democratic model for Egypt. Others proposed a socialist political framework, while others championed an Islamic approach to nation-building.

According to the supporters of an Islamic political framework, both the secular and socialist models had been tried, tested and found hopeless. Only an Islamic approach to nation-building was, in their opinion, most appropriate for a great Muslim nation like Egypt. One of the most influential Egyptian Islamic thinkers and ideologues of the time was Sayyid Qutb. His thoughts have exerted a profound influence on twentieth-century Islam.

Sayyid Qutb Ibrahim Husayn Shadhili was born in the village of Musha, in Upper Egypt. Although his family originally came from the Arabian Peninsula, it was his immediate ancestors who moved to Egypt. A devout Muslim of spiritual and religious feelings, his father earned his living as a farmer. Living under British military occupation at the time, the majority of Egyptians, whether they were wealthy businessmen, poor farmers, uneducated village-dwellers or high-ranking civil servants, supported al-hizb al-watani. This was an Egyptian nationalist party led by Mustafa Kamil (b. 1874-d. 1908 CE) and his associates. As a nationalist and proud Muslim, hajj Qutb actively supported the political activities of this party, whilst working hard to provide a comfortable living for his family.

He had five children, three daughters and two sons, of which Sayyid Qutb was the eldest. hajj Qutb was keen to provide a good education for his son, so he ensured his son committed the entire Qur'an to memory before he was ten. Thereafter, young Qutb studied the life of the Prophet, his companions, and Islamic history. After completing his primary and secondary education, Qutb left his native Musha and, in 1921 CE, settled in *al-Qahira* (Cairo), the capital of Egypt. It was a bustling centre of intellectual, cultural and literary activities.

In Cairo, he lived with his uncle and enrolled at a preparatory college to secure a place at *dar al-uloom* (the present-day Cairo University). It was originally founded by the Egyptian government to train teachers for state schools. This institution offered Westernstyle modern education along with the more traditional disciplines. The Egyptian middle classes were particularly willing to secure places for their children at this institution because this offered a quick route to securing a relatively well-paid government job. Sayyid Qutb was keen to pursue a career in teaching. So he completed his preparatory courses and secured a place at *dar al-uloom* to study for a degree in education.

From 1927 to 1930 CE, he fully engaged himself in his studies and became actively engaged in cultural and literary activities. He became a prolific writer and literary critic while he was still in his twenties. He regularly published articles, reviews and poems in some of Cairo's leading newspapers and journals. His insightful reviews, thoughtful articles and moving poetry soon established his reputation as a leading literary figure. Despite his traditional upbringing, Qutb's writings were almost entirely modernistic and nationalistic in their tone. Nevertheless, he was not a supporter of Western modernism and secularism which was being imported into Egypt from Europe and promoted throughout the country by the Egyptian elite. Indeed Qutb opposed such wholesale importation of Western morals and values.

During this period, he authored his *Ashwak* (Thorns), a love story which ends in tragedy. 'Child from the Village' is an autobiographical account of his early life. In *Madina al-Mashoorah* (The Bewitched City) he presented a literary account of historical buildings and royal palaces. At the time, he regularly rubbed shoulders with prominent Egyptian writers and intellectuals like Taha Husayn, Abbas Mahmud al-Aqqad, Mustafa Sadiq Rafa'i and other great Egyptian writers and poets. By now, Qutb was considered to be a talented writer and literary critic in his own right.

After graduating from *dar al-uloom* in 1933 CE, he taught at local schools before joining the Ministry of Education. Qutb was keen to improve the Egyptian educational system. He drafted many research papers suggesting ways to reform the country's educational policies and practices, but his proposals fell on deaf ears. To add insult to injury, the Egyptian government was only too eager to please the British elites. As expected, this made Qutb very angry. It prompted him to openly criticise the Egyptian government for its slavish attitude towards the British and its failure to reform the nation's young and growing educational system.

Qutb was increasingly considered to be an unpredictable person by his colleagues because of his proposals. His superiors at the Ministry of Education were relieved when he agreed to go to

America – financed by a government grant– to research American educational philosophy and methodology. However, soon after he arrived in America in 1948 CE, he became seriously ill. Being asthmatic, the long and hard journey intensified his breathing problems, but eventually, he made a full recovery and joined Wilson Teacher's College in Washington DC to learn English. He then moved to Colorado and also visited California, Chicago and San Francisco before returning home to Egypt in 1951 CE.

Qutb's stay in America changed his outlook on life forever. As an educated, cultured and sensitive man, Qutb felt American society had very little to offer him. He considered American values and way of life to be riddled with both moral and ethical contradictions. Behind the glitter of material wealth and luxuries, he discovered how the ugly ghosts of spiritual deprivation, moral scepticism and cultural schizophrenia ruled supreme throughout American society. He could not understand why the Egyptian elites were so keen to import such morals and values and promote them in Egypt as products of high culture and civilisation. By sacrificing collectivism at the expense of individualism and spirituality at the expense of material prosperity, American society, he felt, had been gripped by moral relativism, social distrust and economic insecurity. He was convinced that American morals and values were not the answer for a Muslim society. Qutb experienced an intellectual, as well as a cultural, transformation. If his bosses at the Ministry of Education had sent him to America to open his mind to things Western, then he returned to Egypt to become a champion of Islamic values and morality. In his book 'America as I saw it', Qutb demolished the argument that American culture and values were worth copying by the Egyptians. He also exposed the delusions inherent in Western materialistic values and philosophies.

In 1949 CE, while Qutb was confined to his bed at George Washington University Hospital suffering from repeated respiratory problems, he received news of Hasan al-Banna's assassination. After the murder of the Egyptian Prime Minister, Mahmud Pasha (b. 1888-d. 1948 CE), allegedly by a member of *ikhwan al-muslimun* (The Muslim Brotherhood), al-Banna was gunned down on the streets of Cairo by the Egyptian secret service. The Muslim Brotherhood was founded by al-Banna in 1928 CE (see chapter 103). It was a mass Islamic movement which resisted the Egyptian elite's attempts to promote Western morals and values in Egypt. Instead, they advocated the need to promote and implement Islamic morals, ethics and values throughout the country. This movement became so popular, that by the early 1940s, it became too powerful and influential for the liking of the Egyptian authorities. Thus, they initiated repressive measures against its main leaders and activists to undermine the whole organisation. However, the Brotherhood continued to flourish until its founder was assassinated in 1949 CE.

On his return to Egypt in 1951 CE, Qutb closely studied the ideas, thoughts and methods of the Brotherhood, and a year later he formally joined the organisation. Instantly he became one of its most prominent figures, along with Hasan al-Hudaybi. The period from 1949 to 1952 CE was a crucial period for Qutb for several reasons. Firstly, his understanding of and approach to Islam radically shifted during this period. He now began to see Islam in its entirety. That is to say, it was no longer a cultural element in his worldview, but rather he began to see Islam from an ideological perspective. Secondly, convinced that Islam was much more than merely a set of do's and don'ts, he developed an understanding of Islam as a religion, culture and way of life – an all-encompassing worldview.

He developed his conceptual and ideological approach to Islam in several books he authored at the time, including 'Social Justice in Islam', 'Conflict between Islam and Capitalism' and 'Islam and Global Peace'. As a prolific writer and an influential Islamic thinker, Qutb knew very well that writing books alone does not lead to change. One must also be prepared to struggle to translate one's vision into reality. This pushed him into political activism under the banner of the Muslim Brotherhood.

Qutb did not marry; he remained a confirmed bachelor all his life which enabled him to devote all his time and energy to writing books on Islam. He also became an Islamic political activist on a full-time basis. The more Qutb reflected on Islamic principles and practices concerning Egyptian society, the more he became convinced that his country had become engulfed by *jahiliyah* (deviation from Islam) – morally, politically, culturally and economically. He argued that *hakimiyah* (sovereignty) only belonged to Allah and that the Egyptian political and social order had to be changed to reflect that truth. Thus, he encouraged the need for *jihad* (individual and collective struggle) to change the current situation in favour of an Islamic social and political order. The concept of *jahiliyah* and *hakimiyah* played an important role in Qutb's ideological approach to Islam. These terms were first interpreted in a socio-political way during the 1940s by Abul A'la Mawdudi (see chapter 101). Qutb integrated Mawdudi's political ideas to develop his own ideological interpretation of Islam.

As a prominent member of the Brotherhood and one of its chief ideologues, Qutb soon ran into trouble with the Egyptian authorities for promoting the need for Islamic reformation in the country. But Jamal (Gamal) Abd al-Nasir (b. 1918-d. 1970 CE) who assumed power following the overthrow of King Farouk (b. 1920-d. 1965 CE) was determined to steer the country towards a secular path. However, when the Brotherhood began to oppose Nasir's secularist proposals, they were censured by the authorities. Two years later, in 1954 CE, the Brotherhood was banned by Nasir's regime after an alleged attempt on his life by a member of the Brotherhood.

As a result, all the prominent leaders of the Brotherhood were arrested, including Qutb. After a botched trial, he was sentenced to fifteen years imprisonment, during which he authored his monumental commentary on the Qur'an, *Fi Zilal al-Qur'an* (In the Shade of the Qur'an). It is widely considered to be one of the most influential Qur'anic commentaries of the twentieth century. In it, Qutb developed an ideological interpretation of Islamic thought and worldview. It has been translated into English and published in eighteen volumes.

Although released from prison in 1964 CE due to poor health, a year later he was rearrested for actively supporting and co-operating with the Brotherhood. He was accused of advocating the violent overthrow of the government. The authorities made up evidence to prove that he was a threat to the Egyptian government and thus deserved the death penalty. Passages were plucked out of his books, especially his *Ma'alim fi'l Tariq* (Signposts on the Road), to seal his fate. A military court established by the authorities tried and sentenced him to death at the age of around sixty. He walked to his death without any fear or regret. Although Qutb indeed advocated *jihad*, he did not preach violence, nor did he call for the overthrow of the Egyptian government through force. Certain radical groups in Egypt and elsewhere have since tried to justify their violent actions against their oppressive regimes by misinterpreting his ideas and thoughts.

Likewise, some Western writers on Islam and Middle Eastern affairs have wrongly labelled Qutb a 'philosopher of terror'. They claim that Qutb's political and ideological interpretation of Islam provided the intellectual justification for extremist groups like *al-jama'ah al-islamiyah* and *al-Qa'ida* to perpetrate their crimes. To be fair to Qutb, this is a very sweeping generalisation which fails to consider the full thrust and complexity of his religious thoughts and ideas.

What is true, however, is that Qutb was not immersed in traditional Islamic thought and scholarship. Thus, his interpretation of certain aspects of Islam, for example, the concepts of *tawhid* (Divinity), *hakimiyah* (sovereignty), *jahiliyah* (deviation from Islam) and *jihad* (personal and collective struggle) are far from being traditional. In that sense, he was indeed a radical Islamic thinker and activist. However, it would be equally wrong to say that he was an advocate of religious extremism and political violence, as some Western journalists and writers have suggested.

103

Hasan al-Banna
(b.1906 - d.1949 CE) /
(b.1324 - d.1369 AH)

During the nineteenth and early twentieth centuries, a significant part of the Muslim world was colonised by European powers such as France, Britain, Holland and Italy. Although Egypt had been an upholder of Islamic culture and tradition since the beginning of the seventh century, in 1882 CE the British invaded and colonised this important Muslim country. The ruling British leaders maintained a tight political and military grip on Egypt and promoted Western education, culture and values across the country. Being loyal and proud Muslims, the Egyptians resented foreign interference in their internal affairs. Indeed, the Egyptian public considered the British attempt to weaken, liberalise and westernise their country as an open attack on their Islamic identity, culture and heritage. In 1922 CE, the British faced mass opposition and resentment and were forced to grant limited freedom to Egypt, although the Egyptian people continued to campaign for their full independence. Their campaign eventually forced the British authorities to withdraw their forces and leave Egypt.

British occupation of Egypt formally ended in 1936 CE, but they continued to exercise considerable political, economic and cultural influence in the country. The main mission of the Egyptian liberation movement was to throw the British out of their country so they did not attempt to imoppose the spread of secularism and westernisation in Egypt which threatened to create havoc within Egyptian society at the time. The *jami'yat al-ikhwan al-muslimun* (Organisation of the Muslim Brotherhood) was destined to fill this moral and spiritual void. It was founded by Hasan al-Banna. This mass Islamic movement attempted to stop the spread of secularism and westernisation in Egypt by restoring the Islamic ethos, morals and values across the country. In the process, the Muslim Brotherhood became one of the twentieth century's most powerful and influential Islamic movements.

Hasan ibn Ahmad al-Banna was born in the Egyptian village of Mahmudiyah. His father came from a lower-middle-class Egyptian family and attended al-Azhar University, one of the Muslim world's most famous seats of Islamic learning. He earned his living by repairing watches and pursued research in *Hadith* and *fiqh* (Islamic jurisprudence) during his free time. He edited and wrote several commentaries on the works of classical scholars like and Imam al-Shafi'i (see chapter 30) and Imam Ahmad ibn Hanbal (see chapter 31) and, led prayers at his local mosque. Ahmad's personal piety and love of books (he had a large personal library of traditional Islamic literature) inspired young Hasan al-Banna to commit the entire Qur'an to memory as a child.

Heavily influenced by his father, he used to say, 'Islam is my father and I have no other.' After completing his elementary education at home under the care of his learned father, he enrolled at a local government Teachers' Training Centre, where he completed a three-year course. He then applied to join the *dar al-uloom* (Cairo University) to pursue higher education. When he was offered a place at this institution, his family moved to Cairo where, in 1927 CE, he passed his final examinations. Thus, at the age of twenty-one, he took up his post as a teacher at a government school in an area called Isma'iliyah.

During his student days at *dar al-uloom*, al-Banna observed the social and cultural condition of his people very closely and what he saw utterly shocked and horrified him. The mass invasion of western culture, values and habits into Egyptian society, he felt, had severely undermined the traditional Islamic culture and ethos. This was happening at a time when the ruling elites were busy strengthening their political positions while leading Egyptian intellectuals and literary figures like Taha Husayn and Ali Abd al-Raziq were seeking to dismantle traditional Islam. To add insult to injury, the public also began to surrender to the attractions of modernity and westernisation. This was leading to a deliberate disregard for, and violation of, Islamic principles and practices across urban Egypt. When al-Banna was posted to Isma'iliyah, he was surprised to observe how the forces of modernity and westernisation had transformed that locality too. This prompted him to regularly visit the local cafes and shops to invite the locals to return to Islam.

Being neither a theoretician nor an academic, he spread the message of Islam through personal contact. Once, when he was asked why he did not write books, he retorted, 'I write men.' True to form, he soon won the hearts and minds of the locals, thanks to his polished interpersonal skills and eloquence. The people, in turn, came to greatly admire and respect him for his unflinching devotion to Islam.

Soon al-Banna gathered around him a sizeable following in Isma'iliyah. Encouraged by his success, he formally introduced the *ikhwan al-muslimun* in 1928 CE to revive traditional Islamic principles and practices in and around Isma'iliyah. It is not clear, at this stage, whether he imagined this organisation to be a local effort, or the beginning of a nationwide Islamic revivalist movement. Either way, the Brotherhood started as a local association which sought to bring about moral and spiritual reform in Isma'iliyah by inviting the locals, both young and old, men and women, back to the original, pure message of Islam. Al-Banna's experiment proved so successful that people from all walks of life flocked to the Brotherhood.

Then again, such a response was not entirely unexpected because the people of Isma'iliyah – like those in Cairo, Alexandria and other towns and cities of Egypt – had become very angry and disillusioned with the ruling people. The rulers were keen to keep matters the same for their personal benefit, rather than start much-needed political and economic reforms to improve their people's lives, whether they lived in urban Cairo or rural villages. When al-Banna's call for spiritual and moral, social and cultural, and economic and political reform struck a chord with the locals, they became his most passionate supporters, and this encouraged him to plan the Brotherhood's religious philosophy, methodology of *da'wah* (Islamic propagation) and organisational structure.

Unlike Jamal al-Din 'al-Afghani' (see chapter 90) and Muhammad Abduh (see chapter 92), al-Banna was neither a political theorist/activist nor a religious thinker. Rather he was a community activist who directly engaged with the people to bring about individual, as well as collective, change through preaching, advice, and training. Just as his understanding and approach to Islam were comprehensive, the organisation he founded was also inclusive and practical. The Islamic concept of *tawhid* (or Divine Unity), he felt, provided the basis for a moral, spiritual, political, economic and social transformation of society for the betterment of the people. He shunned religious sectarianism and advocated the need for unity and solidarity based on a traditionalist understanding of Islamic principles and practices.

Inspired by the Prophet, his *sahabah* (companions) and the early Islamic scholars and reformers, al-Banna urged his followers and supporters to engage in worship and devotional activities during the nighttime and strive hard to reform their society by following Islamic teachings during the daytime. Since social and cultural change cannot be brought about individually, he encouraged his followers to work collectively under the banner of the Brotherhood. Being a gradualist rather than a revolutionary, he adopted a bottom-up – as opposed to a top-down – approach to social change and reformation.

Indeed, his practical and down-to-earth approach proved hugely successful in Isma'iliyah. So much so that during his stay there he established several mosques, as well as schools for boys and girls. He also set up social welfare organisations and even created employment opportunities for the local people. Six years after its beginning, the Brotherhood became one of the most powerful and active Islamic organisations in and around Isma'iliyah. During this period, al-Banna also found time to marry and start his own family. Most crucially, he kept a detailed diary of his duties and daily activities. As expected, this diary, 'Memoirs of Propagation and Propagator', subsequently became an important source of information about his life and career.

In addition to this, he wrote scores of articles on different aspects of Islam which were later published under the title of 'Articles of Hasan al-Banna'. Also, keen to encourage his followers to purify themselves both physically and spiritually, he compiled a collection of religious sayings and supplications entitled *al-Ma'thurat*. This booklet was published and circulated widely by the members of the Brotherhood.

Al-Banna stayed in Isma'iliyah until 1933 CE when he was transferred to a teaching post in Cairo. By that time, the Brotherhood had expanded beyond his expectations, and new branches began to mushroom everywhere. Eager to co-ordinate the activities of his expanding organisation, he abandoned his teaching career and became a full-time Islamic activist. As in Isma'iliyah, here now in Cairo, he noticed how the people had become angry and dissatisfied with the obedient attitude of the Egyptian political and religious leaders towards the British elites. His call for Islamic unity and solidarity therefore received a favourable response from the public, who flocked to the Brotherhood in their droves. New branches of the Brotherhood were soon established across Cairo so that by 1934 it had established its presence in no fewer than fifty suburbs of Cairo, thus attracting a mass following. At the time, al-Banna's main objective was to counter the popularity of Western culture and values in Egyptian society by calling the masses back to the original, pristine message of Islam.

In so doing he hoped to bring about a moral and spiritual transformation throughout Egyptian society. As a successful grassroots-based organisation, the Brotherhood soon spread across Egypt and won the hearts and minds of the Egyptian people including farmers, students, teachers, doctors, engineers and lawyers. With its increasing popularity, the Brotherhood also expanded its activities in response to the people's diverse needs and requirements.

In 1938 CE, al-Banna prepared a comprehensive programme for the Brotherhood and called for reform in all spheres of Egyptian society in the light of the Qur'an and Prophetic *Sunnah*. As before, his call for educational, social, political and economic reforms went down well with the Egyptian people. Indeed, the Brotherhood's opposition to the British elites, coupled with its desire to create a fully-fledged Islamic state in Egypt, soon won it widespread support across the country. During the period from 1939 to 1945 CE, the Brotherhood became one of the largest and most influential

Islamic organisations in Egypt. In response, al-Banna changed the Brotherhood's organisational structure so that he could coordinate its activities more effectively. By establishing their own mosques, schools, medical clinics, shops, community centres, women's groups, newspapers, magazines and recreational facilities (without any support or assistance from the Egyptian government), the Brotherhood effectively became a state within a state.

Given its wide-ranging services and activities, the command structure of the organisation also became increasingly complex. As the *Murshid al-Am* (Chief Guide) of the organisation, al-Banna worked very closely with a dedicated team based at its *Maktab al-Irshad* (Central Office). The Central Office was responsible for planning the organisation's policies and strategies. The members of the *Maktab al-Tanfidhi* (Executive Office) were responsible for implementing its policies, procedures and guidelines at the grassroots level. Al-Banna created many other layers of command within the Brotherhood to facilitate better communication and effective delivery of its services. His extensive knowledge and understanding of Islam, coupled with his vision, foresight and organisational ability, enabled him to translate the values and principles of Islam at a practical level.

As the Brotherhood became increasingly popular in Egypt, the country's rulers, and especially the powerful British elites and their Egyptian juniors, became very alarmed. Wrongly accused of spreading anti-state propaganda, the authorities first outlawed the Brotherhood's newspapers and journals, including the famous *al-manar* (The Lighthouse) magazine. This was followed by the enforcement of governmental restrictions and censorship on the organisation's religious activities. This led to the forced scattering of its prominent leaders and activists from Cairo. These measures were activated by the government to undermine the Brotherhood, its unity and organisation, but following a huge public outcry, the authorities were forced to give up.

Then, in 1948 CE, the State of Israel was founded in Palestine. This prompted some members of the Brotherhood to spearhead a military campaign against the new country. A year later, the Brotherhood was outlawed by the Egyptian government which led to widespread rioting, as well as the murder of the Egyptian police chief, allegedly by a member of the Brotherhood. In response, the government arrested all the prominent members of the Brotherhood and cut its activities across the country. The crisis eventually spiralled out of control when Mahmud al-Nuqrashi, the Egyptian Prime Minister, was assassinated, allegedly by a member of the Brotherhood.

A month later, al-Banna himself was gunned down on the streets of Cairo, allegedly by the Egyptian secret police. He was forty-three at the time. Although he was succeeded by Hasan Isma'il al-Hudaybi, who was a prominent judge and Islamic scholar, the Brotherhood and its leaders continued to be harassed, persecuted and repressed by all subsequent Egyptian governments. In spite of this, the Brotherhood remains one of the most powerful politico-religious organisations in Egypt to this day. Indeed, its message and popularity have spread across the Arab world.

Likewise, al-Banna's religious ideas and thoughts have influenced some of the most prominent Islamic scholars and reformers of the twentieth century, including Sayyid Qutb (see chapter 102); Taqi al-Din al-Nabhani, the founder of *hizb ut-tahrir* (the Party of Liberation), and Shaykh Ahmad Yasin, the founder of *Hamas* (the popular Palestinian Islamic Resistance Movement) among others.

104

Malcolm X
(b.1925 - d.1965 CE) /
(b.1343 - d.1385 AH)

It is a well-known fact that the African people did not go to North America of their own choice. They were taken there by force. But what is not so well known is that the enslavement of black Africans began as early as the 1640s. This state of affairs continued until Abraham Lincoln, the President of the United States, formally abolished slavery in the Northern States by signing the Emancipation Proclamation in 1863 CE. The Southern States, however, resisted such measures until the tide of history overwhelmed them.

The confirmation of the Fourteenth Amendment granted American citizenship to all former slaves. Two years later, the passage of the Fifteenth Amendment gave them the right to vote. The offer of constitutional rights to the African-Americans represented a fundamental shift in America's attitude towards its black population. However, this did not make much difference to their social, political and economic conditions at the time.

Later, when millions of African Americans began to move to the North in search of a better life, its white population, fearing increasing competition for jobs and housing, rose against the black migrant workers. The Depression years of the 1930s intensified racial tension across America. It led to widespread rioting and racial violence between the whites and blacks in both the Northern and Southern States. Then a Black Nationalist movement which was inspired by Marcus Garvey (b. 1887-d. 1940 CE) swept America. It paved the way for the Civil Rights Movement to emerge during the 1940s. Malcolm X, one of the most charismatic and influential African-American leaders of the twentieth century, rose to fame during this period. He left his permanent marks in the records of modern history.

Malcolm X was born Malcolm Little in Omaha in the State of Nebraska. He was the son of a Baptist Minister. His father, Reverend Earl Little, and his mother, Louise, were active members of Marcus Garvey's Universal Negro Improvement Association (UNIA). Despite being on the receiving end of white racism and violence, his parents worked hard to improve their social and economic conditions. Later the Ku Klux Klan (a white supremacist group) forced his family to leave Omaha and settle in Lansing, Michigan. Malcolm was only a youngster at the time. Here the family struggled to overcome their social and economic difficulties. Their situation was worsened by Earl Little's drinking habits, which often created tensions within his family.

When Malcolm was six his father died. This again forced his family to experience more difficulties. The challenge of raising nine children on her own proved too stressful for his mother who later had a mental breakdown and was confined to a psychiatric institution. Like his brothers and sisters, Malcolm was brought up in foster homes. He enrolled at Mason Junior High School in Lansing, where he completed the eighth grade. At school, his white teacher urged him to become a carpenter since becoming a lawyer, in his opinion, was an unrealistic aspiration for a black boy. Malcolm quit formal education in disgust.

From Lansing, he travelled to Boston where he was surprised to discover how the black working-classes had become content with the very little wealth they had accumulated. He felt that the ideals which had inspired generations of black nationalists and freedom fighters had been forgotten by the black working classes who at the time lived in the suburbs of Boston and New York. Happy with their share of material benefits and comforts, he thought these people were no longer willing to fight for the cause of Black Nationalism like the previous generations. This state of affairs troubled young

Malcolm, even though he was not in a position to do anything about it at the time.

During this period, he visited Boston and New York regularly. The urban black working-class neighbourhoods became his favourite hideouts. He was then sucked into the murky world of drugs and crime. He soon became a seasoned street hustler and the leader of a gang of thieves. He established his reputation as a fearsome leader of the local criminal group. The one-time 'Detroit Red' — a nickname given to him for the reddish colour of his hair — was eventually arrested. He was found guilty of armed robbery and imprisoned for six years. He soon experienced a life-changing transformation.

After years of criminal activity, he now began to think about his life, its meaning and purpose. He also began to ask questions about the higher things in life. He was keen to explore these issues so he read books on history, philosophy, culture and religion. During this time, he became something of a hermit and read avidly with the result that his eyesight became strained and he began to wear glasses. Reading widely enabled Malcolm to explore and understand the true nature and complexities of human life, culture and civilisation. So, whilst still in prison, his brother introduced him to the teachings of Elijah Muhammad (b. 1897-d. 1975 CE) and the Nation of Islam.

Elijah was the son of a Baptist preacher from Georgia. He established the Nation of Islam. This was a religious and black nationalist movement during the 1930s. Elijah was inspired by Wallace Fard Muhammad (b.1877-d. 1943 CE). Over time the movement became a hugely controversial, but powerful force within the African-American community. According to Elijah, the white people were devils created by black scientists. Fard Muhammad was the incarnation of Allah. His racialistic interpretation of Islam was rejected by mainstream Muslims but Malcolm found the tone and confidence of his message attractive. As a religious and nationalistic movement, the Nation of Islam was a highly organised and disciplined organisation which championed the rights of marginaliszed black people.

Having experienced much racism and hardship at the hands of the white supremacists, Malcolm found in the Nation of Islam a social and religious movement which was not afraid to speak up for the rights of black people. Indeed, the Nation of Islam was not only a champion of Black Nationalism; it also advocated a form of black supremacy over whites. This proved most attractive to Malcolm who became very fond of Elijah and the Nation of Islam while still in prison.

As expected, on his release from prison in 1952 CE, Malcolm became an active member of the Nation. Furthermore, his determination to recruit more marginaliszed and downgraded blacks to the Nation met with instant success. As an eloquent orator and great motivator of people, he took the message of the Nation directly to the people. His success won him much-needed recognition and praise from the Nation's hierarchy, including Elijah himself. His hard work, coupled with his untiring energy and commitment to his task, soon saw him rise from being an unknown assistant Minister of the Nation's Detroit Temple Number One to its national spokesman within a short period.

Most interestingly, when Malcolm first joined the Nation in the early 1950s, it had no more than several thousand followers. But, under his able leadership, the Nation of Islam became a powerful mass movement with more than a hundred thousand loyal followers. He regularly visited the black ghetto areas of Detroit, Boston and New York and urged the poor and marginaliszed black people to join the Nation and fight for their rights and liberty. The locals responded to his call very positively. By the 1960s the Nation of Islam had more than forty temples in various cities. Moreover, it owned several local radio stations which, in turn, enabled them to reach yet more people.

Thanks to Malcolm's sharp intellect, electrifying oratory skills and charismatic personality, the Nation of Islam's image of being a fringe fundamentalist group soon changed for good. Also, when his high-profile attacks on the root causes of economic inequality, social deprivation, political powerlessness and cultural ghettoisation of the African-Americans struck a chord with the masses. As a result, his popularity hit an all-time high. His 'tell it as you see it' approach soon turned him into a cult figure within the black communities. By the same token, his frank and outspoken attack on the ruling classes began to anger the establishment. It was not long before the right-wing American press began to brand him 'the angriest black man in America'.

According to his critics, Malcolm was a racist who preached a fabricated, confused message of racial supremacy, religious hatred and cultural separatism. He was not discouraged by such criticism and continued to champion the cause of the poor and dispossessed black people. Unlike Martin Luther King Jr. (b. 1929-d. 1968 CE), whom he considered to be a 'chump, not a champ', Malcolm became a voice for millions of voiceless African-Americans who had been suffering economic hardship and social deprivation for many generations in the ghettos of major cities of America.

By contrast, the Civil Rights Movement led by Martin Luther King Jr., hardly made any difference to the lives of the poor and disadvantaged African-Americans of the South. But Malcolm's call for black liberation, economic self-help and political empowerment instantly captured the imagination of his fellow black Americans in the North. Indeed, under his stewardship, the Nation of Islam became a very powerful and influential voice for America's black public.

As Malcolm's popularity continued to rise, Elijah Muhammad became concerned by the increasing politicisation of the Nation of Islam. Since he considered himself to be a religious leader rather than a politician, he was not too keen to get involved in politics and public affairs. Although Malcolm's loyalty to Elijah was absolute, Elijah's non-political stance on many important issues of the day disappointed him. A furious and uncompromising Malcolm was itching to go out and openly advocate the need for black resistance if that was what was required to achieve real liberation and freedom for the African-American people.

However, his fusion of religious passion with political activism horrified a laidback Elijah, who started seeing Malcolm as a liability rather than an asset. Soon afterwards, Malcolm commented on a news report about the assassination of John E Kennedy. The comment was the final straw which broke the camel's back. Elijah considered it to be an insensitive comment and banned him from speaking in public. During this period Malcolm became aware of Elijah's mismanagement of the Nation's finances and his involvement in extra-marital affairs. This horrified him and prompted Malcolm to leave the Nation of Islam in 1964 CE. It was not an easy decision for him but the moral and financial corruption which prevailed under Elijah's leadership left him without a choice. After leaving the Nation, he and his supporters initiated two separate organisations., The Muslim Mosque, Inc., and the Organisation of Afro-American Unity (OAAU). The former was essentially a religious institution and the latter became the political wing of the Muslim Mosque.

Thereafter, Malcolm travelled across Africa and the Middle East. He also performed the sacred hajj where he experienced yet another life-changing transformation. For the first time, he came into contact with mainstream Muslims. His experience of the universal brotherhood of humankind championed by Islam captured his imagination. In response, he openly rejected Elijah's distorted and racialistic interpretation of Islam and became an orthodox Muslim. From then on, he became known by his new Muslim name, El-Hajj Malik El-Shabazz. From Makkah, he wrote many letters wherein he explained the reasons why he had had a change of heart. He spelt out his new thoughts and ideas on race relations, human rights, cultural co-existence and social and political issues. On his return to America, he began to champion mainstream Islam and advocated the need for both racial and cultural tolerance and understanding across all sectors of American society.

Furthermore, he developed an internationalist approach to human rights and Third World politics. He became an advocate of social equality, economic justice, political independence and freedom for the world's poor and dispossessed people — especially his fellow African Americans. Unfortunately, he did not live long enough to develop his thoughts on these issues systematically. He fell prey to an assassin's bullet on February 21, 1965 CE, three months short of his fortieth birthday.

As a result, three Nation of Islam loyalists were arrested. They were found guilty of his murder. However, it is not clear whether the Central Intelligence Agency (CIA) or the Federal Bureau of Investigation (FBI) played a role in his assassination. According to some of his biographers, the CIA and FBI did play a part in his murder. This view has not been proven. Thankfully, just before his death, Malcolm had completed his autobiography. It was published immediately after his death. *The Autobiography of Malcolm X* provided a detailed account of his life in his unique style.

In the final analysis, Malcolm X was a truly revolutionary leader. He became an undisputed champion of America's poor and disadvantaged black people. He did so by the force of his extraordinary character and personality. Today, he is not only considered to be one of the founding fathers of the anti-racist movement, but he was also one of the most influential Western Muslim leaders of the twentieth century.

105

Muhammad Yunus
(b.1940 - CE) /
(b.1359 - AH)

When the early Muslim traders first arrived in the coastline regions of India in the seventh century, they were welcomed with open arms by the locals. Though these pioneering Muslims came primarily to conduct business, over time they married and settled in some of the most remote coastal towns of India, Ceylon, Sumatra and Maldives. When Ibn Battuta (see chapter 73), the celebrated fourteenth-century Muslim globetrotter, visited those areas he was surprised to find thriving indigenous Muslim communities in all the major coastal regions of India, Ceylon and Sumatra. He was particularly struck by the wealth, prosperity and kindness of the people of Bengal, especially Sylhet and Chittagong (in present-day Bangladesh).

At the time, Chittagong was one of the leading seaports of the subcontinent where Muslim merchants came regularly from Yemen to conduct business. This city not only became a commercial hub for the early Muslim traders, but it also became a prominent centre of *Sufism* (Islamic spirituality). As the home of one of Bangladesh's largest seaports, Chittagong has remained a thriving centre of trade and commerce to this day. Muhammad Yunus, one of the most radical economists of contemporary times and arguably the single most influential banker and social businessman of his generation, originated from this age-old centre of commerce and spirituality.

He was born and brought up in a lower-middle-class Muslim family. Young Yunus attended his local schools where he studied Bengali language, literature, mathematics and science. He grew up during a politically unstable and culturally confusing time in the history of the subcontinent. The Second World War had started in 1939 CE and the British - who still maintained their grip on India - had joined the war in Europe. As an integral part of British India, East Bengal also faced an imminent military invasion from the Japanese who were making rapid progress in the East. To make matters worse, the people of East Bengal were, at the same time, passing through a period of considerable social and cultural conflict and confusion.

What did it mean to be a Bengali Muslim? Should the people of India remain loyal to the Crown during a difficult period in British history, or should they rebel? What would happen to the Indian Muslims if the British decided to quit? Could the Hindus and Muslims live side-by-side in a free and independent India? Yunus spent his early childhood in the heart of Chittagong's commercial district at a time when the people of India, especially its large Muslim minority, were asking themselves such politically significant and culturally relevant questions.

As it happened, the British had no choice but to quit India in 1947 CE after agreeing to Muhammad Ali Jinnah's demand for a separate homeland for the Muslims of India. Yunus was only seven at the time. The Muslims of East Bengal, which later became known as East Pakistan (1947-1971 CE), were delighted with the outcome, although Yunus was too young to understand and appreciate the significance of this historic event. As a talented student, he excelled in his studies and completed his further education at Chittagong College before proceeding to Dhaka University for higher studies. After graduating from Dhaka University in 1961 CE, he lectured on economics at Chittagong College. Then he won a Fulbright scholarship to read economics in the United States. He left his native East Pakistan and moved to the United States to research in economics at Vanderbilt University in Tennessee. In 1972 CE he returned to a new country – now named Bangladesh – with a doctorate in economics.

As a Bengali nationalist, Yunus was happy to see Bangladesh appear on the world map. As an economist, he was keen to help his new country re-organise its crumbling economic structures but, according to Yunus, the country's leaders were not very keen to utilise his skills. Following a brief time at the planning commission, he became a professor of economics at the University of Chittagong in 1972 CE.

While he was busy teaching economics, Yunus observed, to his utter shock, the disturbing impact of horrible poverty around the villages adjacent to the university campus. He could not understand why the locals did not make better use of their agricultural land, which remained uncultivated season after season. The villagers' failure to use fertile land did not make economic sense to Yunus. He was not an agriculturalist, but he was very keen to discover why the locals did not grow crops, fruits and vegetables which they could consume and also sell. From 1972 to 1976 CE, he explored different ways to improve the economic condition of the local villagers. As a result, he established small farming and irrigation projects to improve the use of the local agricultural land. While working on these projects, he discovered that the wealthier farmers tended to dominate their poorer ones.

Moreover, making the local villagers completely dependent on their land did not seem to him to be a good idea either, because he had yet to identify the real causes of their economic backwardness. Although the main purpose of these projects was to help the poor to become self-reliant and independent, Yunus's failure to address the root causes of poverty made him rethink his research method and objectives. During his research, and also drawing on his practical experience of delivering small agricultural projects, Yunus came up with the idea of lending small amounts of money to the very poor to encourage them to set up small businesses. The borrower was required to repay the sum, plus a minimal amount of interest, over some time out of the profits generated from the business.

Pioneered by Yunus in 1976 CE, this method of lending small sums of money to some of the world's poorest people became known as the 'system of micro-credit'. The normal financial system refused to give loans to people who had no fixed assets. He felt the poor could never obtain loans from the banks because they had no valuables. So, the question of where the poor could go to obtain small loans needed to be resolved.

In his attempts to obtain bank loans for the poor, Yunus discovered that conventional banks automatically excluded the very poor from receiving any form of credit. This prompted him to set up the Grameen ('village') Bank experiment in 1977 CE to provide credit to the poor, especially to the women, in rural areas of Bangladesh. By giving out such loans he hoped to encourage women to set up small-scale businesses and self-help projects, and in so doing, enable them to stand on their own two feet and gradually improve their social and economic condition. In theory, the concept of micro-credit seemed to be a commendable one, but it was not clear whether it would work in practice. In Yunus's own words:,

'At first, I did not know if I was right. I had no idea what I was getting into...learning as I went along, learning empirically from experience. Our work became a struggle to show that the financial untouchables are actually touchable, even huggable. To my amazement and surprise the repayment of loans by people who borrow without collateral is much better than those whose borrowings are secured by enormous assets. Indeed, more than ninety-eight per cent of our loans are repaid, because the poor know this is the only opportunity they have to break out of poverty.'

When in 1979 CE he was granted a two-year break from teaching at Chittagong University, he replicated the Grameen Bank scheme in a poor part of Tangail, outside Dhaka, the capital of Bangladesh. When the experiment proved a success, Yunus and his colleagues organised the micro-credit self-help programme in other areas of Tangail. From then on, the Grameen Bank gradually expanded across rural Bangladesh so that today it has more than nine million borrowers across Bangladesh. One may ask, what is so unique and special about the Grameen Bank? First, the Grameen Bank is nothing like a conventional bank. A conventional bank's basic operating principle is, 'the more you have, the more you get.' and conversely, 'If you don't have it, you don't get it.'

In other words, the conventional banks have labelled the poor people to be 'not credit-worthy', that is to say, 'we can't touch you'. Therefore, the conventional banks have created a kind of financial apartheid, argues Yunus in his inspirational autobiography, 'Banker to the Poor: Micro-Lending and the Battle Against World Poverty'.

However, the Grameen Bank has turned this basic banking principle on its head because it does not operate on the premise of security. That means the very poor who have no land or assets of their own can obtain micro-credit loans from the Grameen Bank to set up small businesses or self-help initiatives to improve their socio-economic condition and boost their morale, confidence and self-esteem.

The system of micro-credit pioneered by Yunus back in the 1970s has not only proved to be a great success in rural Bangladesh; the concept has since been successfully replicated in more than 100 countries around the world including the United States, United Kingdom, Canada, France, Australia, Malaysia, China, India, Pakistan, Norway, Finland and across South America. Currently, the microfinance model pioneered by Yunus is serving more than one-hundred million around the world with around twenty-five billion dollars of loans.

Unsurprisingly, the system of micro-credit has been praised by some of the world's most powerful leaders and global financial institutions (including the World Bank and the International Monetary Fund (IMF)) as an important tool in the fight against abject poverty and deprivation. Though Yunus studied conventional economics in a conventional way, his understanding of economics is surprisingly unconventional; rather, it is very radical indeed. In his acceptance speech for the World Food Prize, awarded to him in 1994 CE, he stated, Brilliant theories of economics do not take into account issues of poverty and hunger. They tend to imply that these problems will be solved when the march of economic prosperity will sweep through the nations. Economists spend all their talents detailing the processes of development and prosperity, but none on the processes of poverty and hunger. I feel very strongly that if the world recogniszes poverty alleviation as an important and serious agenda, we can create a world that we can be proud of, rather than feel ashamed of, as we do now,.

Yunus's radical approach to economics in general and poverty reduction in particular was initially rejected as being simple-minded and unworkable by his critics at the World Bank and other global financial institutions. But, by turning the Grameen Bank into a successful venture, he proved all his critics wrong. In July 2005 CE, total loans disbursed by the Grameen Bank topped $5 billion. The

Grameen Bank today distributes more rural loans each year than all other Bangladeshi banks put together. It has also established more than 2500 branches across rural Bangladesh in more than 80,000 villages with a workforce of nearly twenty-five thousand. The bank currently distributes more than twenty billion dollars in loans to over eight million borrowers, with ninety-seven percent of them being women. By all accounts, this is a truly great achievement. According to Yunus, poverty is an example of a cancer which humans have created and forced upon their fellow humans. It is so widespread because political oppression, economic inequality and social injustice are common in many parts of the world.

Moreover, the way international trade and business are conducted plays a major role in the production of poverty in the Third World. For this reason, Yunus's pioneering effort to tackle abject poverty through micro-credit schemes deserves more support and recognition from both politicians and the world's leading financial institutions than it has received so far. However, one of the reasons why Yunus's micro-credit scheme has not been as popular in the Muslim world is because it is *riba* (interest or usury) based scheme. Since interest-based transactions have been outlawed by the Holy Qur'an, many Muslims have understandably refused to support such a scheme.

Nevertheless, poverty – both relative and absolute – can only be eradicated when the world's most powerful leaders and financial institutions make poverty eradication their priority. This will not happen until the world's prominent leaders are prepared to tackle the root causes of global inequality and injustice by addressing the imbalances and inequalities which exist in international trade between wealthy Western nations and poor Third World countries. In other words, according to Yunus, poverty will not be completely eradicated until the restrictive practices which support the structures of global economic inequality and injustice are first dismantled.

Nevertheless, the pioneering concept of micro-credit of Yunus has made a significant contribution to the global fight against absolute poverty and deprivation. He is also the author of several bestselling books including 'Creating a World without Poverty' and 'Building Social Business: The New Kind of Capitalism that Serves Humanity's Most Pressing Needs'. In addition, he is the founder and chairman of Yunus Centre, a social business think-tank based in Dhaka, which works to alleviate poverty and develop sustainability, both in Bangladesh and globally.

In recognition of his outstanding contribution and achievements, Yunus has been awarded scores of prestigious international prizes and awards, including the Noble Peace Prize in 2006 CE, the Presidential Medal of Freedom from the United States in 2009 CE and the Congressional Gold Medal in 2010 CE, as well as fifty honorary doctorates from universities around the world. In 2012 CE, Yunus was also named by Fortune Magazine as one of the greatest entrepreneurs of modern times. In 2024 CE he became the leader of the interim government of Bangladesh.

106

Muhammad Ali
(b.1942 - d.2016 CE) /
(b.1361 - d.1437 AH)

If the Islamic contribution to philosophy, mathematics, science, arts and architecture is not widely known in the Muslim world and the West, then the Muslim contribution to international sports has received even less recognition. This is most unfortunate given the fact that some of history's most famous and influential sportsmen have been Muslims. Thus, internationally famous sportsmen like the French footballing legend Zinedine Zidane; the American basketball superstar Karim Abd al-Jabbar; the Pakistani cricketing star Imran Khan; and the celebrated North African athlete and long-distance runner Nuredine Mousalli and, former Wimbledon doubles champion Sania Mirza were all Muslims.

Their contribution to the world of competitive sports was both unique and exceptional. On an equal footing with these remarkable sporting stars, Muhammad Ali, the legendary American boxer and philanthropist became, during his career, the undisputed king of the ring. He was widely considered to be the most famous sportsman of all time. He was one of the most influential boxers in history. He was arguably one of the two most famous people of his generation, along with Nelson Mandela (b. 1918 - d. 2013 CE), the former South African President and legendary freedom fighter.

Muhammad Ali was born Cassius Marcellus Clay Junior., in Louisville, Kentucky, into a working-class African-American family. His father, Cassius Senior., and his mother, Odessa, were a hard-working couple. They, like any other parents, tried to provide the best for their children. Young Ali inherited both the sweet, bubbly and steadfast qualities of his mother. He also inherited the fast-talking, creative qualities and attributes of his artistic father. Ali and his younger brother Rudy grew up in the happy but conservative environment of Western Louisville. At the time it was a predomi-nantly black area. The white areas of the city were strictly 'no-go' areas for its black population so the Clay family's movements were restricted to the city's black areas.

Like many other parts of America, the racial segregation of Louisville was characteristic of the wider racial and cultural seg-regation which plagued American society at the time. As a young-ster, Ali was known to have been both shy and reserved. Thanks to Rudy and Joe Elsby Martin, a local police officer, he soon became interested in sports. According to Ali, when he was about twelve, his father bought him a new bike for Christmas. It was stolen from him by thieves. This prompted an unhappy Ali to go to Joe Martin to make a complaint. Joe compiled a police report and asked Ali to join him at his Columbia Boxing Gym.

A tall, slim and shy Ali went to the gym and put on his box-ing gloves for the first time. His agility, athleticism and frighten-ing speed impressed Joe Martin. Joe asked him to attend his gym regularly. Keen to improve his boxing skills, Ali began to take extra lessons with his brother Rudy, who trained him by hurling stones at him, to improve his reflexes. He learnt to evade with ease. If Joe Martin introduced Ali to boxing, then Fred Stoner would become his first serious boxing instructor. As a respected black boxer him-self, Stoner taught Ali the art of boxing rigorously and systematical-ly. Stoner considered Ali to be highly gifted and encouraged him to develop his stamina, technique and speed, something all aspiring professional boxers had to master from the start.

Young Ali's ability to move with ease, dance around the ring and deliver crushing blows to his opponents with frightening speed soon convinced Stoner that he was a great boxing talent. Stoner knew that Ali could reach the heights of sporting stardom. Ali con-firmed Stoner's prediction when he was barely sixteen by winning the Louisville Golden Gloves lightweight tournament. Whilst still in high school, he progressed to the quarterfinals of the regional boxing championship in Chicago. Then, after graduating from Louisville's Central High School at the age of eighteen, he won the National Golden Gloves tournament. He also won the Amateur Athletic Union competition. His achievements at both local and national level included a further six title fights. These established his reputation as an emerging star.

Thanks to his success, Ali was chosen to represent his country at the Olympics in Rome in 1960 CE. He won a Gold Medal which made him instantly famous. He was aware of his achievements, good looks and electrifying personality. He was also in the habit of bragging about his boxing ability and greatness even when he was a youngster. And no one (including his parents, trainers and fans) ever doubted his physical ability, boxing talent and way with words. Those who knew the eighteen-year-old Ali described him as inspiring, energetic and sophisticated. After returning home from Rome with an Olympic Gold Medal, a group of white millionaire businessmen came together and formed the Louisville Sponsoring Group. This was a business group which sponsored and promoted his fights.

He signed a profitable contract with this consortium and began his professional boxing career at the age of eighteen. Sponsored by the company, he fought his first professional fight in 1960 CE and scored a sixth-round victory. His emergence as a professional boxer created considerable interest in the sport. His flashy style, self-confidence, imagination and arrogance also turned him into an overnight celebrity. He was keen to show the world that he was not a one-time wonder. So he approached Angelo Dundee, a renowned boxing trainer, to join his team and supervise his training needs and requirements. The two men soon became good friends and Ali flourished under Dundee's coaching.

During this period, he trained hard, mastered his footwork and became a polished boxer. His physical power, coupled with his lightning speed, agile movement and quick-thinking made him a formidable boxer. In 1962 CE, he thoroughly mesmerised and beat Archie Moore. The press and the American public were bowled over by the quick-witted, boastful and ferocious Ali. He was now increasingly considered to be one of the most entertaining boxing sensations of his generation. In reality, however, Ali had barely started his professional boxing career.

Nevertheless, his convincing victory over Moore opened the way for him to challenge Sonny Liston (b. 1032-d. 1970 CE), the then-reigning heavyweight champion of the world. Ali, the challenger, entered the ring with Liston in 1964 CE. He chanted 'Float like a butterfly, sting like a bee', and demolished the feared and revered Liston. By combining his unconventional boxing skills with his colossal punching power, Ali stunned the American public by becoming the heavyweight champion of the world. Before the fight, Liston predicted, 'I might hurt that boy bad', and every American believed him (including the press, the public and the pundits). But a confident and arrogant Ali, then only twenty-two, proved them all wrong. After soundly beating the world heavyweight boxing champion, he emerged to proclaim, 'I am the greatest!'

The year 1964 CE represented an important period in American history. It marked the beginning of a decade of student protests under the banner of the Free Speech Movement. In the same year, the American army was given the green light to attack Vietnam. The white supremacists affiliated with the Ku Klux Klan began to terrorise famous Civil Rights activists in Mississippi and, of course, the Beatles took America by storm. But it was Ali's historic victory over Liston in 1964 CE which represented a high point in the history of global sporting achievement. Even before the dust of his victory over Liston could settle, he announced that he had converted to the Nation of Islam. This represented another shock so far as the mainstream American press and public were concerned.

No one expected Ali to out-smart Liston, but he proved his critics wrong. Then, to add insult to injury, he announced his conversion to an organisation which was widely considered to be a racist, black-separatist movement. As expected, soon after his conversion to the Nation of Islam, Ali's career and public image took a battering from the American press. He felt mainstream America had failed to understand him. He felt that his conversion to Elijah Muhammad's Nation of Islam was far from being a moment of madness. He was taught and mentored by none other than Malcolm X (see chapter 104). He closely studied the Nation's religious thoughts and method for more than a year before formally becoming a member.

His change of religion was a real change of heart and belief. It was not a publicity show. He was encouraged by Malcolm X, Warith D. Muhammad and Elijah Muhammad to change his name to Muhammad Ali. Ali no longer wished to be known by his 'slave name'. Like him, tens of thousands of other African Americans found true freedom, liberation and self-respect in the fold of the Nation of Islam. During this period Ali married for the first time and continued to box. He allowed his fists to do all the talking inside the ring. He not only retained his heavyweight championship title by defeating Liston for the second time in 1965 CE but also successfully defended the title another six times in 1966 CE, with five knock-outs.

A year later, another public protest broke out. Ali refused to sign up for military duties in Vietnam. As a conscientious objector, he responded to his critics in rhyme. 'Keep asking me, no matter how long. On the war in Vietnam, I sing this song. I ain't got no quarrel with the Viet Cong.' He was found guilty of draft evasion by an all-white jury. He was fined ten thousand dollars and sentenced to five years in prison. He was freed on appeal but his boxing licence was suspended. He was also stripped of his World Boxing Association (WBA) title. At a time when his promising boxing career appeared to be in ruins, a determined Ali remained as firm as ever. During this period, he married for the second time. Three years later the Supreme Court quashed his conviction for draft evasion.

He responded by returning to the boxing ring with a bang. He won two successive bouts before losing against Joe Frazier. But he regained his title in 1974 CE and successfully defended it against Frazier a year later in the 'Thrilla in Manilla'. Ali's autobiography entitled '*The Greatest My Own Story*', which he co-authored with Richard Durham, appeared in 1975 CE. Two years later, Ali married for the third time. In the following year, he fought one of his most memorable bouts against George Foreman in the famous 'Rumble in the Jungle' in Zaire. It earned him five million dollars.

He then lost against Leon Spinks. But he regained his title for the third time and in so doing he became the only man to have won the world heavyweight championship three times. After two more fights — one against Larry Holmes in 1980 CE and the other against Trevor Burbick in 1981 CE – Ali finally retired from boxing in 1981 CE at the age of forty-one. He fought a total of sixty-one bouts. A few years later, he told the New York Times Magazine that he was suffering from Parkinson's syndrome, probably as a result of repeated blows to the head. As a result, he developed speech problems even though his mental faculties were not affected. Ali made more than fifty million from boxing and gave away a substantial amount to fund charitable activities. In other words, after he retired from boxing, he became one of America's most prolific philanthropists and charity workers.

Moreover, as a sporting legend and a distinguished statesman, he went to Lebanon in 1985 CE and Iraq in 1990 CE to secure the release of hostages from those countries. In addition, as a charity and humanitarian ambassador, he travelled around the world delivering food and medication to the poor and needy including as far as Indonesia, Morocco, Sudan and Liberia. He patronised and proactively supported numerous charities and humanitarian organisations, raising millions of dollars for much-needed and worthy causes. He was particularly supportive of some of the world's most vulnerable and oppressed, especially the Palestinian people.

In recognition of his high-profiled and wide-ranging charitable and humanitarian work, he received numerous awards including the 'Lifetime Achievement Award' from Amnesty International. He was named 'International Ambassador of Jubilee 2000'. He received the Presidential Medal of Freedom in 2005 CE. The Secretary-General of the United Nations also recognised him as the 'United Nations Messenger of Peace'. Furthermore, Ali was honoured by the Kings of Saudi Arabia and Morocco for his services to Islam.

Thanks to Ali's efforts, the Muhammad Ali Centre for the Advancement of Humanity (now known as the 'Muhammad Ali Center'), consisting of a six-storied building, was unveiled in his hometown of Louisville, Kentucky in 2005 CE at the cost of eighty million dollars. It comprises a museum and resource centre. It organises talks, seminars and exhibitions on Ali's six principles of confidence, conviction, dedication, giving, respect, and spirituality. These promote cultural understanding and shared values, not only for Americans but also for the betterment of the whole of humanity.

In 1991 CE, Thomas Hauser published his popular biography of Ali under the title of *'Muhammad Ali: His Life and Times'*. Robert Cassidy's definitive study *'Muhammad Ali: The Greatest of All Time'* was published eight years later. However, one of the most memorable sporting images of recent times was that of an unwell Ali carrying the Olympic torch in Atlanta in 1996 CE. The public story of this great sportsman culminated in the release of Micheal Mann's Hollywood film blockbuster *'Ali'* in 2001 CE. It featured Hollywood superstar, Will Smith. In 1999 CE, *Time* magazine named him as one of the '100 Most Important People of the 20th Century'. The BBC recognised him as their 'Sports Personality of the Century', in addition to numerous other awards and honours.

On a more personal level, Ali had married four times. He had two sons and seven daughters. He died on June 2, 2016 CE, at the age of seventy-four. His memorial service, held in his native Louisville, Kentucky, was broadcast live, thus attracting an estimated one billion viewers worldwide.

Glossary

Imran Mogra

Asceticism – see *zuhd*.

Austere – living with no luxuries, strict in manners, having a plain appearance. See *Zuhd*.

Batini – hidden, any doctrine which is inner and secretive. It also refers to someone who belongs to a group with such beliefs. It also refers to doubtful doctrines.

Bedouins – nomadic Arabs living in the deserts of the Arabian Peninsula and across North Africa. The word Bedouin is from the Arabic word '*badawi*' meaning desert dweller. Most are animal herders, but many have abandoned their tribal traditions for urban lifestyles.

Caliph – in Arabic *Khalifah*, a successor of Prophet Muhammad who took responsibility and ruled on behalf of Allah and his messenger. The plural for *Khalifah* is *Khulafa*.

Caucasus – the land of Sultan Muhammad Uzbeg Khan of the Golden Horde, a mountainous area between the Black Sea and the Caspian Sea, includes parts of Russia, Georgia, Azerbaijan, Armenia, Turkey and Iran. It has the highest peaks in Europe.

Chishtiyah – an important and famous spiritual *tariqah* (path) named after a famous Sufi of India, the saint Shaykh Muin al-Din Chishti. See Sufi Orders.

Creed – a set of systematic beliefs that influences the way a person lives, or a statement of faith.

Dar al-uloom – lit. a house of knowledge; an Islamic seminary for higher education in Islam.

Exoteric – *zahiri* meaning external in contrast to esoteric (*batini*) meaning inner.

Falasifah – philosophers, *falsafah* is Arabic for philosophy.

Fiqh – lit. to understand; the study of Islamic law and jurisprudence. A specialist in Islamic law is a *faqih*, a scholar, sometimes called *Imam*. The plural is *fuqaha*.

Gnosis – spiritual awareness, knowledge of Allah, experiential knowledge. See *ma'rifa*.

Hasan – lit. good; a category of *Hadith*. See *sahih, mawdu*.

Hijaz – meaning the barrier; the region of current Saudi Arabia. It is bordered in the west by the Red Sea, in the north by Jordan, in the east by the Najd and south by the Asir.

Ijtihad – lit. to struggle, make the greatest effort; refers to the use of reason to find an appropriate ruling on a matter not directly ruled by the Qur'an. It is an intellectual effort.

Irfan – synonymous to Sufism, it is recognition of Allah, being very close to Allah. See *ma'rifa*.

Ishraqi – from the Arabic *ishraq* meaning illumination; a follower or philosopher of the school of philosophy of Shaykh Shihab al-Din Suhrawardi. See Suhrawardiyya, Sufi Orders.

Jurisprudence – *fiqh*, law, Muslim legal system, there are four main schools (*madhhab*) of jurisprudence among the Sunni communities.

Jurist – an expert in law, a person trained in *fiqh* and *Sharia*. See *faqih*.

Kalam – lit. speech; applied to Islamic theology which is the study of Divine Speech. These theologians were called *ahl al-kalam*, Imams or scholars of *kalam* or *mutakallimun*.

Khanqah – see Zawiyah.

Khwajah – an honorific title meaning master, mainly used for Sufi teachers.

Mahdi – lit. the guided person; the one to appear before Qiyamah to return righteousness.

Mahasabha – Hindu Mahasabha, a Hindu nationalist organisation and political party.

Mantiq – lit. logic or speech; a science whose principles protect from making errors. It involves studying definitions and proofs. It enables accurate and clear thinking. It has three parts: conceptualisation, judgement and reasoning.

Metaphysics – is a major work of Aristotle. In it he developed the doctrine of First Philosophy. It is one of the greatest philosophical works and its influence on the Greeks, the Muslims and other philosophers was huge.

Mongols – warriors from Central Asia who swept through Islamic lands in the 13th and 14th centuries causing massive destruction. The most famous were Genghis Khan, Hulago and Timur.

Mufti – a legal official who may be an assistant to a *qadi* (judge) or be a *qadi*. They have the authority to decide about important religious matters faced by Muslims. See *fatwa*.

Mystic – a person who follows a spiritual path or Sufi Order for self-purification. See Sufism.

Mysticism – the inner dimension, a path for spiritual knowledge and purity. See Sufism.

Neoplatonic – this is a philosophical system which started after Plato and is grounded in the teachings of Plotinus. It argued that this world is only a copy of an ideal reality which lies beyond this material world.

Orthodoxy – the generally accepted beliefs which do not depart from the original tradition. See heterodoxy.

Pan-Islamism – the plan of unifying all Arab states into one United Arab Republic. Pan-Islam the idea of unifying all Muslim states. Many Muslims favour a return of the Madinah ideal, the creation of the Kingdom of Islam, led by caliph for all Muslims.

Peripatetic – a philosophical school which follow broadly the Greek tradition. It involves thinking while walking. Plato would invite his student Aristotle for contemplative walks.

Persia – This is ancient Iran. The term Persia was used for centuries, mainly in the West, to designate those regions where Persian language and culture dominated. The region of modern Iran. The Persian language is also known by Farsi or Parsi.

Philosophy – it is a form of rational and intellectual inquiry, it aims to be systematic, it tends to critically reflect on its own methods. The study of knowledge, reason, language and existence.

Qadi – usually a judge appointed by a ruler or a government on the basis of the extensive knowledge of Islamic law. The decision of a *qadi* is final.

Qadiriyah – an important and famous spiritual *tariqah* (path) named after a famous Sufi of Baghdad, the saint Shaykh Abd al-Qadir al-Jilani. It is popular from India to Morocco. It is also known as Jilalah in the Arab West. See Sufi Orders.

Rationalism – a school of thought which applied reason to the solutions of philosophical problems. See Mu'tazila.

Reformist – Muslim responses to modernity by using different approaches like traditionalist rejectionists, modernist and secularist. Muslim reformers addressed modern culture with Islamic traditions. Links to the Arabic word *islah* means to reform, to fix, or revive.

Secularism – opposes religion, separates state and religion, it is a political idea of how to govern a state, it defends all civil liberties, it is not atheism.

Seljuks – a dynasty of a Turkic people (1037-1194 CE), their ancestral leader was Seljuk (Saljuq), their Oghuz clans converted to Islam in the eleventh century.

Shadhiliyah – an important and famous spiritual *tariqah* (path) named after a famous Sufi Shaykh Abu al-Hasan al-Shadhili, followed by millions of people around the world. See Sufi Orders.

Sufi lodge – usually a place of religious retreat. See Sufism, Zawiya.

Sufi Order – a path of guidance to spiritual purification and character development to get closer to Allah and develop His love. There are many methods (Sufi Orders). See Naqshbandiyyah, Chishtiyah,

Murabitun, Qadiriyah, Suhrawardiyya, Tijaniyya and others. See Sufism.

Sufism – in Arabic *Tasawwuf*, probably derived from *safa* meaning purity or *suf* meaning wool (simple garments). Sufism is often called Islamic mysticism or spirituality. It emphasises purification of the *nafs*, heart, mind, actions by developing piety, devotion, religiousness, *zikr*, and constant awareness of Allah. See Sufi, Sufi Order.

Tafsir – to explain and give commentary on the meaning of the verses of the Qur'an.

Tasawwuf – Islamic spirituality. See Sufism, Sufi, Sufi Order.

Theology – the study of the nature of Allah and religious beliefs from a religious point of view.

Tijaniyah – an important and famous spiritual *tariqah* (path) named after a famous Sufi Shaykh Abu al-Abbas Ahmad al-Tijani (1737-1815 CE). It is widespread in Morocco, Algeria and sub-Saharan Africa. See Sufi Orders.

Ulum al-aqliyah – philosophical sciences like logic, mathematics, philosophy and medicine.

Viceroy – a ruler exercising authority in a colony on behalf of a sovereign, e.g., Viceroy of India during the British Empire.

Zahiri – meaning literal and apparent; a school of law which adopts literally meanings as opposed to allegorical or mystical interpretation of texts. Now almost extinct.

Zawiyah – In North Africa, it means an oratory or small mosque, a meeting place for Sufis for prayer or *zikr*. It may be a small or large or even a mausoleum of a saint. It is equivalent to *khanqah* in the East or *tekke* or *dargah* in Turkey. Also, part of a room set aside for prayer. See Sufi lodge.